2 I AM, THEREFORE I THINK

I AM, THEREFORE I THINK

OTHER BOOKS BY THE SAME AUTHOR

God Consciousness, The Journey Of A Science Driven Psychic Medium

Spiritual Sight, The Manual (Co-authored with Melvin L. Morse, M.D.)

I AM, THEREFORE I THINK

A psychic medium's insights into the emergence of consciousness in the universe

By Isabelle Chauffeton Saavedra

Survival of Consciousness, LLC

This is a non-fictional book. It includes aspects of science (quantum mechanics and cosmology), which have been carefully reviewed by physicists, but which do not constitute a scientific body of work. All opinions and views expressed in this book, are solely those of Mrs. Isabelle Chauffeton Saavedra, and do not represent the views and/or opinions of the scientific community, or the views and/or opinions of the various authors and scientists, whom Mrs. Chauffeton Saavedra is quoting in the book.

Text copyright © Isabelle Chauffeton Saavedra
All rights reserved. Published in the United States by Survival of Consciousness, LLC.

Visit us on the web: www.survivalofconsciousness.com

Facebook:
https://www.facebook.com/Isabelle.c.Saavedra.SurvivalofConsciousness/

And:
https://www.facebook.com/groups/survivalofconsciousness/

Printed in the United States of America

ISBN-10: 0-9984887-0-4
ISBN-13:978-0-9984887-0-7

In memory of my Dad, Jean Chauffeton
Your love for science and mathematics has always inspired me. I just wish I were as brilliant as you are. I can only try to follow in your footsteps and be the best I can be.

CONTENTS

	Acknowledgment	Page 11
	Introduction	Page 13
	Prologue	Page 15
1.	Science: A Paradigm Shift	Page 17
2.	The Point of View of the Experimenter	Page 26
3.	Why Must There Be a Why?	Page 33
4.	Let's Explore the Why Part 1: Cosmology and Us	Page 43
5.	Let Explore the Why Part 2: Quantum Mechanics and Us	Page 56
6.	Oh, My God!	Page 80
7.	Consciousness and the Universe(s)	Page 87
8.	How Does Consciousness Express Itself?	Page 92
9.	Subconscious Brain vs Conscious Brian	Page 102
10.	Consciousness First or Human Brain First?	Page 106

11. Properties of Consciousness   Page 117

12. To Be or Not to Be   Page 123

13. Is Consciousness Truly Retrievable Data?   Page 129

14. How Is Consciousness Processed Through the Brain?   Page 146

15. Do We Have Free Will Over Consciousness?   Page 152

16. Is Consciousness Responsible for All the Deeds and Events in the universe(s) and on Earth?   Page 163

17. Can Consciousness Heal the world?   Page 170

18. I Am, Therefore I Think   Page 180

    Photos   Page 184

    Bibliography and sources   Page 186

    About the author   Page 190

ACKNOWLEDGEMENT

I would like to express my deepest gratitude for their invaluable help in the process of writing this book, to the following people and friends:

Melvin Morse, M.D. who has been a friend and a mentor for many years. You have challenged me to my core in the writing of this book and it has brought me to another level of understanding of the process. For all your countless hours of editing, mentoring and your friendship, thank you.

Lisa Brull who has been a friend for almost twenty years. Your careful and attentive proofreading and suggestions have helped me tremendously. For your precious time, and for being so nice and gracious, thank you.

I also want to thank my physicist friends who have advised me throughout the book, helping me keep my science facts straight, while letting me speculate in unchartered territories. All of your joint expertise has been a crucial guidance and support to me.

INTRODUCTION BY MELVIN MORSE M.D.
BEST SELLING AUTHOR OF "CLOSER TO THE LIGHT"

Isabelle Chauffeton Saavedra's latest work "I Am Therefore I Think" represents an exciting breath of fresh air in the tired "skeptical scientist vs fervid believer" debate that has dominated consciousness studies for the past fifty years. She rejects the reigning metaphysical model which divides spiritual and physical reality and reunites science and spirit. Scientists can now embrace their spiritual side and faith based individuals can be reassured that their deepest intuitions are validated by science.

She proposes a startling new model of consciousness that builds on modern information theory as well as the ancient wisdom of Tibetan monks and early Western physicians such as Paracelsus. Her vision is breathtaking as she seamlessly integrates the work of modern astrophysicists such as Paul Davies PhD with the conclusions of ancient masters of consciousness research such as Siddharta Gautama (the Buddha) and his followers. She ushers in a revolutionary era of scientific mediumship at the same time as creating a new paradigm for understanding modern physics and spirituality.

Fritjof Capra, over twenty-five years ago in the Tao of Physics, stated that to truly understand the universe, we needed input from both theoretical physicists and experts in spirituality. Ms. Chauffeton Saavedra continues that necessary dialogue with this outstanding book.

Prologue

As physicists reflect on the origin and the expansion of our universe, and theorize on all the possible interpretations of mathematical equations describing its modus operandi, one thing seems to often evade their approach: their very own human limitations.

Is "nothing goes faster than the speed of light" a true fact of the universe or a shortcoming of our observational and interpretive skills limited by experimental design?

In quantum mechanics, Schrodinger's experiment forces us to conceptualize a cat being dead and being alive at the same time, in two most diametrically opposed, yet simultaneous, states of existence.

However, it is not something we are typically ready to digest as we are still struggling to come up with a language that can describe the surrealism of quantum physics.

Yet, there is a world filled with wonder and incredible beauty that we can't see beyond the horizon. It is inaccessible due to the limitations of our very own perceptions.

For example, near-death experiencers (*NDErs) have seen this world and even they struggle to describe it with traditional language.

Once we realize that there is a way to pierce through this veiled reality using the only tool we have, our brain, we will use new pathways never before scientifically acknowledged and we will truly unleash an infinite potential; the potential of understanding our own interaction with the universe and our relationship with our fellow conscious beings in all their possible states of existence, including death.

*An NDE (near-death experience) is first the action of having been declared clinically dead by medical professionals, during a significant amount of time, then of having experienced visions and sensations while being clinically dead, and finally of having been resuscitated with medical techniques or having come back to life spontaneously. Upon their return to life, some near-death experiencers tell stories of verifiable facts that they remember happening (including out-of-body experience – OBE) while their hearts were no longer beating and their brains were no longer functioning, they were thus incapable of producing and exhibiting vital function.

Chapter 1
SCIENCE: A PARADGIM SHIFT

"I think, therefore I am"
— Mathematician and Philosopher René Descartes

René Descartes created a revolution in mathematics and philosophy when he wrote those now famous words in the mid 17th century.

Although he had briefly studied medicine, he had very limited knowledge and understanding about the physiology of our brain and its role in creating awareness.

Yet, his philosophical statement left a tremendous impact on science.

His theory was that all truths were connected. If one knew one fundamental truth, all the other truths could be found by deduction or logic.

In his "Discourse on the Method", he laid the foundation of mathematical and philosophical rational thinking and causality. However, he admitted that what led him to this scientific path of study were three visions and dreams he had. Due to poor health, he would stay in bed until mid-morning and would use this time to consciously meditate. Descartes was very much like a pioneer, an edgy scientist who was not afraid to use all the tools and skills that nature and the universe had given him.

But what made him a "celebrity" was his famous phrase:

"I think, therefore I am."

He coined the phrase after realizing that everything that had been said before was either wrong or not quite right.

To him, the best course of action was to erase everything and start at the beginning. The only certainty he was left with was: "I exist". Based on that affirmation, he created a path of thinking built upon deduction and logic.

Three hundred and fifty years later, the fundamentals of our education are still based on his principle. Our world is still focused on explaining reality with the rational thought processes created by our brain; more precisely by the left-brain part of our mind-brain unit.

"*Left Brain*" *is a neuroscience-based metaphor widely used to define the logical, ego-based, rationally and language powered functions of the mind-brain unit. The left side of the brain typically handles those functions. In the same style,* "*Right Brain*" *is a neuroscientific metaphor used to characterize the non-verbal, artistic, musical, intuitive and sensory-based behaviors of our brain. These functions are mostly generated by the right side of our mind-brain unit. Neuroscientists commonly use the term* "*Mind-Brain*" *to define the intricate relationship between the physical brain and the mind*". - Dr. Melvin Morse in 'Spiritual Sight, The

Manual' Co-written with Isabelle Chauffeton Saavedra.

During the millions of years of human evolution, the different humanoid branches leading to our species have advanced with one single goal: explaining and understanding what we think "reality" is to survive and thrive.

We have done a pretty good job, as it seems we are indeed at the top of the food chain. Although technically speaking we are not at the top of the food chain as we don't eat the meat of all the animals below us, however, our scientific development allows us to kill any other species in order to survive.

We have established our presence on this planet thanks to the development of our brain, which has more than tripled in size according to the data gathered by scientists. The brain of the Australopithecus who roamed East Africa four million years ago weighed just about a pound, whereas the brain of the Homo Sapiens, the human species as we know it today (dated about 200 000 years ago) weighs in at about three pounds of gray matter. Scientific studies have associated the increase in the mass of the brain with the use of more sophisticated tools found at the sites of each specimen unearthed.

Many a paleontological study has overlooked the importance of social interaction, emotional and artistic development in the increase of brain size. By doing so they have reduced the brain to a functional tool that merely exists to ensure our survival.

"I think, therefore I am."

Today, neuroscientists understand that both left and right-brains have an importance in the perception of our reality. It is also known that thoughts and experiences can change the very physical structure of the brain. Until now though, what science has done in a very Cartesian way is to establish that without a functioning brain, there is no "I am".

Yet, is that really true?

The development of science in the modern world has overpowered our lives since the beginning of the industrial revolution in the 18th century. It continues to shape our education system and scientific research today.

The principles of science state that a theory must be proven or disproven, which is the core principles of our understanding of the universe we live in.

But in the case of consciousness, as physicist Dr. Michio Kaku points out *"There has been over 20 000 papers or so written on the subject of consciousness and no consensus. Never in the history of science have so many people devoted so much time and produced so little."*

However, in the last ten years or so, we have been noticing a new type of scientist being born.

This new generation of physicists, such as indeed Dr. Michio Kaku, and neurosurgeons like Dr.

Eben Alexander or Dr. Jean-Jacques Charbonnier, has accepted to look at the brain and consciousness in a new light.

These scientists describe the brain as a very sophisticated type of processor, or sensor. In the case of Dr. Eben Alexander the brain no longer acts as the creator of our consciousness, but rather processes it. For Dr. Michio Kaku consciousness can be quantified with units. To Dr. Kaku, "consciousness is what helps us create a model of our position in space, in relation to others and to time using constant feedback loops". In doing so, consciousness creates our view of reality instead of the brain passively perceiving reality. *(A feedback loop or the feedback of a system, is a process by which a system undergoes modifications following changes of that system's parameters).*

In Dr. Kaku's model, a thermostat may have one unit of consciousness (perceive and analyze temperature), a flower may have ten units of consciousness (perceive and analyze temperature, weather, humidity, gravity etc.) and the bigger the brain (processor) the more advanced level of consciousness. A reptilian brain would be at level one consciousness (x units of consciousness) having great ability in spatial positioning for example, while a mammalian brain would be at level two (y units of consciousness, with y >x), showing great ability in social positioning. And finally, the human brain would be at level three consciousness (z units of consciousness with z > y+x), as it is able to project itself into the future.

In the seventeenth century, Galileo proposed a heliocentric model of our solar system. His friendship with Cardinal Maffeo Barberini who eventually was elected Pope Urban VIII in 1623 did not suffice to appease the political and religious resentment that his new theory had stirred up and he was condemned for heresy by the Catholic Church in 1633. Things haven't changed much since then.

In the same fashion, these brave modern scientists are inclined to revisit the archaic views of consciousness and ready to face the establishment with new ground breaking theories. But they are often poorly received by the scientific community and the public, both anchored in their traditional views and convictions.

These models which have all my attention describe a functioning brain not as the creator of the "I am", but rather as a facilitator of the "I am" to manifest. In another words the brain manifests reality but does not create it.

If Descartes were born today, he would probably say, "I think therefore I manifest". In today's world of neuroscientific knowledge, his understanding of rationality coupled with his propensity to meditate and dream would most certainly have led him onto a different conclusion than "I think, therefore I am".

Certainly, thinking and reasoning in terms of planning in time are indeed prime activities associated with human brain functions. Without a functional brain, we cannot think, we cannot exert ourselves to manifest who we are.

In this book, however, I will examine whether the existence of "I am" depends on our brain, is derived from our brain functions or is a completely independent phenomenon. I will propose new ways of looking at our existence completely independent of our bodily and vital viewpoints.

Two people will interpret a piece of information two different ways. Each person will manifest his or her own reality through the interpretation of that piece of information in a unique way determined by a number of different factors such as her genetic code, her social upbringing, her emotional and physical state at the time of interpretation. Yet, there is an ultimate true information, stripped down from any interpretation; and it includes the information of me, unfiltered.

Thus, I will propose that the "I am" In "I think, therefore I am" (meaning "I exist"), is not the unique result of a thought process, but the consequence of a preexisting consciousness which is manifested by a body and a brain. This is a model in which consciousness does not depend on the brain for its existence and survival.

We are so lucky to be living during this time of scientific paradigm shift. This is only the beginning of an exciting adventure that will take our human species through the maze of a new field of research which treats consciousness as an independent phenomenon.

Science is slowly accepting that a functional brain is not essential for the creation of consciousness. A functional brain is obviously key to the manifestation of consciousness but perhaps not in creating its existence. If, as according to Dr. Kaku, a thermostat can actualize consciousness, then consciousness is something that is manifested but not created, as obviously, a thermostat is not creating consciousness.

Super computers and quantum computers have already shown that even emotions can be interpreted in a logical way and answers involving extremely complex human behaviors can be delivered faster than the speed of light.

However, these computers are only the reflection of our human interpretation of consciousness. They apply processes they have been programmed to do. They are created by our knowledge and rendition of reality.

The reality created by a machine or a brain is not dependent on the existence of either, neither is the consciousness needed to interpret that reality. A non-functional brain, such as in the case of comatose people or persons with cognitive disabilities or illnesses simply prevents consciousness to manifest fluidly.

Yet scientific and experimental evidence points to the fact that a functional brain does not imply the creation of consciousness but its existence and the possibility it is expressed and manifested by the brain-body.

Chapter 2
THE POINT OF VIEW OF THE EXPERIMENTER

"While you are experimenting, do not remain content with the surface of things"
— Physiologist Ivan Pavlov

From my point of view as a scientific medium, I have little to no doubt consciousness exists before the brain exists.

I am a trained psychic medium. I know it is a scary term for scientists, I know it does not call for blind trust from the scientific community. However, science refers to a system of acquiring knowledge. This system uses observation and experimentation to describe and explain natural phenomena. As such, I am a scientist.

I have been experimenting with consciousness for over two decades. As a trained psychic medium, I have done many readings for many clients. Most of my clients wish to connect with a deceased loved one. Some are interested in finding a lost piece of jewelry while others wish to connect with a cognitively disabled loved one. In all cases, each and every reading I do, while a true labor of love on both parts, is also an experiment.

As a science driven medium, there is always a part of my left-brain that will question the validity of the information that comes through during readings.

It's inevitable, because I am human and because that's what my brain, the Homo Sapiens' brain, has evolved to do. It is a question of survival. It is anchored in my limbic brain.

Over the years, I have learned to tame that part of my brain so that it would not interfere (too much) with my readings.

As an experimenter, I have come to the realization that though our brain is not a perfect machine, it's all we have to communicate with our universe and what's around us.

Communicating with the universe is a two-way situation. From the point of view of human nature, my brain and body receive information, and in return send signals back out to my immediate environment. These signals travel a long way. In fact, as with any energy pattern, these signals go on and never die.

Every day, every minute and every second that pass, our brain filters the information it captures and tries to make sense out of it. Every second, our body and brain are bombarded by billions of bits of information in the form of waves of energy and electromagnetic patterns (that we then interpret as sound, colors etc.), as well as cosmic radiations, and maybe even by other forms of data we might not recognize or understand with our current state of scientific knowledge.

All this data is part of the fabric of the universe. All of it is imprinted on a giant hard drive that has been expanding since the dawn of time to accommodate the ever-growing bank of new data.

From these billions information bits, we are showered with at any given time, only about eleven million are utilized every second by our five (known) senses, and relayed to the final sensory integration areas in our brain. In the same amount of time, the brain only end-processes fifty bits of this information. In a whole day (twenty-four hours), our left-brain will process a few tens of thousands of bits of information; the ones necessary, from a rational standpoint, to identify, qualify and quantify our environment so as to give us the unique sense of knowledge and awareness which ensures our bodily survival. In the same time period, our right-brain accesses millions of bits of information but does not process the data to create a version of reality as does the left-brain. This is known by neuroscientists as the right-brain sensory stream of information, accessed but not processed by the brain as a whole.

Most of the information passing through our right-brain is discarded as our left-brain has learned since our youngest age to "take over" everything. *"The left side of your brain can process information bits in a linear or lateral manner. In other words, the information is processed from tiny parts and to whole of it. When a person has left centric brain, [she] collects and collates tiny bits of information, aligns them in a linear manner and organizes all the bits into a logical sequence. On the contrary, the right-brain does not accept information in bits and pieces. It always treats the information as a whole and it starts processing from top to bottom."* Left brain vs right-brain – Understanding the basic difference by Andrew Loh. www.brainy-child.com

Yet, when it comes to filtering information in terms of capacity and diversity, our right-brain is much better armed for it, as it has the capability to retain much more data as it sees global patterns of information as a whole experience.

If we could look at our brain from the point of view of a fisherman, it would look a little like this:

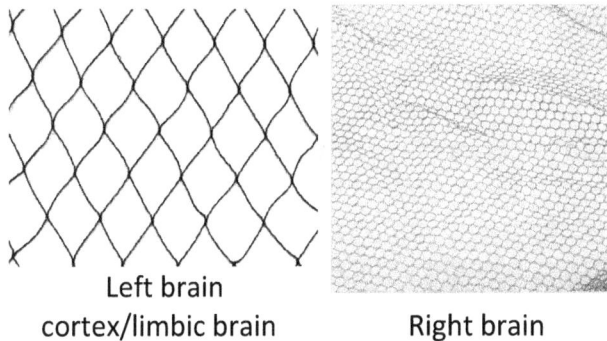

Left brain
cortex/limbic brain

Right brain

As cosmic fishermen, we might use the big net to catch the big fish in the pond ("is there immediate danger? Look! Here, there is food to satisfy my appetite; this job will help me provide shelter to my family" etc.)

However, if we want to catch the multitude of small multicolor fish out there we need to use the smaller, tighter mesh ("The colors of this painting are incredible, I love my children more than anything in the world, this melody makes me cry, wow, wow, wow this is so beautiful…").

As a medium, I do all my séances at a distance without any contact with my clients during the readings. Typically, I do not know anything about them except their name. I determine the date and time of the séances unbeknownst to my clients. Once I have worked on their case, I send them an email with all my findings. My approach is simple; I wish to have no contact with my clients and they do not know when I do their reading to avoid any pollution in the process. I try to get as close as can be to scientific double-blind conditions. In doing so, I increase the validity of the information I receive during the séances.

When I do a reading, the information I receive comes in the form of sensory perceptions such as images, sounds, tastes, smells as well as distinct physical sensations and emotional reactions. A courtesy of my right-brain filtering the information.

Meanwhile, my relentless left-brain tries hard to find meaning to the information gathered by using memory, analogy and acquired systematic knowledge. One pitfall for any trained psychic medium is to let the left-brain take the lead.

To be able to process more information, one has to un-learn the millions of years of accumulated intelligence forged through genetics and acquired knowledge.

Paradoxically, the key to understanding what's around us is to first refuse to explain anything and to rather observe everything with a different set of eyes, from all possible angles, and to refrain from any interpretation.

My role as the experimenter, as small as it may be, is to help demonstrate that the theories of this new generation of scientists are indeed true. I do this by providing the raw data of what actually occurs in the human brain with regards to consciousness, through detailed empirical observations of my sessions and by carefully analyzing their results.

These different theories propose that consciousness is not the byproduct of brain activity but rather that consciousness autonomously preexists everything. This theorizes that consciousness is a stand-alone cosmic and quantum phenomenon that can be filtered through our brain, interpreted and delivered in the form of human actions. (As well as sentient and conscious actions by deductions, thus including the plant and animal kingdoms, and perhaps even the mineral world.) Schematically, consciousness according to these modern scientific theories, is information and data imprinted on the hard drive of the universe's fabric. Our human brain is one of the many possible motherboards bringing the information forth and processing it.

Consequently, following Descartes's reasoning, if the universe were a complete empty vacuum then consciousness would not exist. Yet according to modern quantum physics theory, even in the vacuum of space, an energetic quantum dynamic field does exist, and is the substrate of all realities. This energetic field in fact self-generates data, i.e. information. The information of a vacuum is data; hence the vacuum is never really empty in substance and form.

Modern cosmologists have speculated on what existed before the Big Bang that created material reality in all its forms. Thus, the idea that consciousness must have existed before the beginning of our universe becomes relevant.

The next chapters will attempt to look at this supposition from many different angles. We will first try to explain why we even have to find a reason for our existence and for our cognizance. As we progress in our discovery steps, we will then get a glance of some of the most prominent scientists' visions about how and why the universe and we, sentient humans, came about.

As we go on, we will use the information we will have acquired to reflect on the true nature of consciousness and on the way we interact with it.

Chapter 3
WHY MUST THERE BE A WHY?

"My brain is only a receiver, in the universe there is a core from which we obtain knowledge, strength and inspiration. I have not penetrated into the secrets of this core, but I know that it exists."
— Physicist Nikola Tesla

Why do we humans have to explain everything? Why can't we accept, "there is" without a cause or effect?

For one thing, to accept that "there is" without a cause or effect is to live in the present, which we humans have trouble doing.

Right now, there is me existing in this moment. There is no reason for me to be here, just as there is seemingly no reason for the universe to exist. It just is. To my knowledge, we are the only species on our planet which tortures itself with the "why" question.

As a human species evolving into the Homo Sapiens model, we have become aware of the inevitability of our bodily death, not through the survival instinct that all living beings possess, but thanks to (or because of, I should say) our intellect.

That realization sparked in our ancestors the question that keeps haunting us to this day: "why?"

It seems that no other species on Earth are so preoccupied by the "why" and live a life filled with an accumulation of millions of instants. Each instant is as important as the next or the previous one. For most of the species on Earth, time does not seem to exist in the same form we humans conceive it. Earth species follow patterns, but are not aware of time in the way that we are. They follow the routine of nights and days, the rhythm of the seasons but they have no preconceived ideas of the significance of those patterns. They accept this order of things as it is.

For the dog owners reading this book, go outside for fifteen minutes or go away for three days and your dog will welcome you back like you had been gone an eternity, with the same intensity in the demonstration of what seems to be pure "dog happiness".

We humans have been given a brain that acts like a double-edged sword. One side cuts deep into the understanding of our surroundings and helps us project ourselves in the future, the other side cripples us with questions, which can overwhelm us.

If our universe was born as a reason for something, what could that reason be? Physicists know that one very important law of the universe is that of causality, or in simple terms action-reaction. Everything in the universe follows that rule.

As the universe has been expanding at a faster rate than expected in early research, physicists have been wondering what is causing this acceleration. In fact, they have already determined that dark matter and dark energy combined, invisible to us but which account for about 96% of all matter and energy in the universe, are contributing to this acceleration. These invisible forces create a counter effect against the pull of gravity by massive galaxies and celestial objects leading to a rapid expansion of the universe. We have here a well-established relation of cause and effect.

However, what is the cause of the creation of the universe?

It seems that causality at time zero is impossible to understand or determine, as all laws of physics break down at the point of origin of the universe called the Singularity. We will explain what the Singularity means further down in this chapter.

We have no data, we cannot observe, nor deduce what the cause would be for the creation of the universe before this infinitesimally small point of matter/energy, the Singularity, expanded into the Big Bang. We have no cause for the existence of this point of origin.

What we have, however, is a set of retrofit equations, which gave birth to the concept of a Big Bang; a moment when all conditions were met for the universe to expand. Yet no equations exist to describe the beginning of the existence of the universe.

We are limited by our inability to peer beyond the "observable universe", whose limit is about 378 000 years after the beginning of the Big Bang. This is when electrons and protons started to bind to one another to create hydrogen atoms, releasing photons in the process. Before that, the universe was a hot soup of plasma so dense, light would not come out. So, everything before that is pretty much based on theoretical and mathematical concepts.

These observational limits, which have always been present in our theories of how the universe was created, be they in antiquity or in modern times, have always, naturally and inevitably pushed us to recreate a model that we feel comfortable with, i.e., a human model. A model in which all is encompassed and nothing necessitates explanation: An unknown force or entity, an "external God" creator of the universe.

We invent an external God(s) that answers all our questions. There must be a God, so we think, that created the universe, space and time and he/she is mighty and powerful. This external God is a projection of our inner fears and anxieties, which addresses the question of why we live and die. He/she protects us and also can destroy us at will. While it gives a false sense of understanding it seems to temporarily erase the tormenting effects of the "why" question.

But, really, isn't this shoving the dust under the carpet? If God(s) created everything, who/what created God(s)? If time started when God created the Singularity, then all laws of physics should also have started at that point. However, we know that they didn't exist at the point of Singularity and only started to appear when the inflation (large and fast expansion) of our universe started. We will also describe what the inflation is later.

To understand this barrier, we have to understand what the Singularity is. The Singularity of our universe is a point of volume zero where all the matter and energy of the entire universe is condensed. This would be just before the Big Bang. The problem is that the density of this point of volume zero would be infinite, which would render the laws of physics inoperable. Because of this, scientists have deduced that time (and space) did not start with the Singularity but with the Big Bang.

Let's first make sure we clarify what the Big Bang is. The popular misconception of the Big Bang (that I too had, before revisiting it for this book), is that it is a big explosion from a tiny point of matter. The Big Bang was not an explosion; it is a mathematical construction in which all conditions for the expansion of the universe are met. When astronomer Fred Hoyle introduced the term in 1949, he used it to explain that there was not in fact a "big bang", but that it was a time when the mathematical conditions existed for an expansion of the universe as well as the beginning of the laws of physics as we now know them. The Big Bang was then followed immediately by the Inflation phase, where the universe expanded exponentially fast for a fraction of a second.

What is expansion? The universe's expansion is the action of enlarging, following a certain set of equations relative to space-time that focus on the radius of the universe or the average distance between cosmic objects. It is called the Scale Factor.

Often times cosmologists use the analogy of a rising raisin bread to explain the expansion. If you bake a rising raisin bread in the oven, the whole loaf will expand with the raisins inside of it. The raisins are getting farther from one another but are not moving relative to the dough.

Another example is to place paper clips on a rubber band. If you pull the rubber band in two different directions, it is going to expand. The paper clips will get farther from each other as you pull the rubber band, but they will remain in their same position relative to the rubber band itself. That's what happened with our universe and is still happening.

The universe during its inflation epoch expanded faster than the speed of light; in fact, it expanded in an exponential way. That is mainly due to phase transitions of the quantum soup that constituted our universe back then (A phase transition is a thermodynamic transition between different states of matter like from liquid to gas or from solid to liquid. In the case of our universe, these phase transitions created an exponentially expanding volume in an extremely short time.). To understand why our universe expanded faster than the speed of light we have to remember that the speed of light seems to only be a limit within the universe itself not "outside of it". So, nothing seems to go faster than the speed of light inside the universe, but it does not mean that the universe itself was unable to expand faster than it at the beginning. In fact, it's exactly what it did!

As we briefly talked about earlier in this chapter, because the expansion was so fast and the original plasma was so dense the light within the expansion was not able to get out of the "rising universe's loaf". That's why we have no clear physical image of what happened until only about 378 000 years post Big Bang when the universe started to really cool down.

So how do we know how things happened before that, since the inflation that we are talking about is supposed to have happened a tiny fraction of a second after the beginning of the Big Bang?

We know because the physical image of the cosmic microwave background radiations dated back to 378 000 years post creation shows us a very uniform universe in terms of temperature and radiation. The only way the universe could have become uniform as such a scale was by having hugely expanded extremely fast first, before cooling and continuing its expansion in a slower motion. What are these cosmic microwave background radiations (CMB)? They are the first pictures we have of our universe thanks to the first light that came out when the universe cooled down and atoms started to form, letting light travel freely. At this time of recombination, that is when the first primary atoms of hydrogen, helium and lithium were created, the universe had already acquired an almost universal uniformity.

For those who like numbers, the universe increased it size in a 10^{26} factor (that's 10 with 26 zeros behind it) in less than 10^{-35} seconds (that's 1/10 with 35 zero behind it) and grew roughly from the size of a proton to the size of a grapefruit in that tiny fraction of a second.

I think I hear some of you saying, "well, that's nothing! From a proton to a grapefruit?" In fact, on a cosmic scale, this is an enormous expansion.

Take the size of our sun and compare it to the size of our Milky Way galaxy. The ratio of the diameter of our galaxy to the diameter of our sun is 8×10^{11} to 1. If a grain of sand of 1 millimeter of diameter were our sun, our galaxy would then be 800 000 km in diameter (roughly twice the distance Earth-Moon). From 1 mm to 800 000 km is "only" a ration of 8×10^{11}. The rate of expansion that happened during inflation is 10^{26}, that is 10 followed by 26 zeros. This happened in 10^{-35} seconds. That means 1 second divided by the number 10 followed by 35 zeros! So, imagine how huge the grain of sand would have become! Now do you see it? This happened in the tiniest fraction of a second. Inflation was incommensurably huge and fast!

Convinced now? Just to finish being clear on the notion of expansion vs explosion: If you take a regular explosion (nuclear or TNT), you will never achieve that level of uniformity. In other words, the universe underwent an extraordinarily rapid expansion, faster than the speed of light, but it did not explode in order to make that happen.

So, thanks to today's observations we know that the universe is still expanding and that the expansion is actually accelerating. We seem to have a sound understanding as to the creation of the Big Bang. The combination of our observations and theoretical equations gives us a convincing image of what our universe must have looked like right before (going back in time) the zero point, a tiny fraction of a second before the Singularity.

However, we still don't have an answer as to "why" the universe exists!

Because of that major obstacle, many a theory has emerged to try and explain the beginning of the universe and find a "why", a causality.

These theories are all equally fascinating and all have one thing in common: They all depend on our interpretation of theoretical equations. They are all sort of valid, although some interpretations have become the favorites of prominent physicists.

What does this mean "our interpretation of theoretical equations?" It is our personal way of processing the information through our own brain. As each brain is unique, each interpretation will be too. Each individual will gravitate to one theory or another depending on their own unique set of personal circumstances, meaning that a scientist will perhaps believe one interpretation and a faith based person yet another. Simply put, the scientist has no better insight than a spiritual faith based person with regards to the reasons for the creation of the universe. However, we know that the equations and their mathematical information is the same for everyone. So, it does not really matter what the interpretations are saying, because the original information is true. The math is true.

That original information is spread out in the very fabric of the universe in an ontological way and any attempt at interpreting it is but a quest for the answer to the "why" question.

Thus, in our search to find a reason for our universe's existence, we find ourselves delving into the depth of our own psyche. We wonder how our own observations and interpretations impact our reality and the way we actually understand our universe and ourselves. We hope that in finding a reason why and a modus operandi of how our universe came about, we will unravel the mystery of our own sentience; a state of existence that we can only experience through our consciousness.

In order to fully grasp the ramifications and interconnections between, our consciousness, our collective consciousness and our universe, we need to take a little scientific detour through the different proposed models of our universe as interpreted by some of the most famous cosmologists and quantum physicists in our next two chapters.

Chapter 4
LET'S EXPLORE THE WHY
<u>PART 1 – COSMOLOGY AND US</u>

"The real voyage of discovery consists not in seeking new landscapes, but in having new eyes."
— Marcel Proust, French author

"I'm sitting on the dock the bay, watching the tide roll away [...]" Don't you catch yourself sometimes singing this great Otis Redding song? Wondering about the vastness of the ocean, just sitting and watching the horizon, trying to guess what is behind it figuratively and metaphorically? We always give our horizon of perception some sort of mystical limit beyond which an allegoric world exists that is filled with mystery, enchanting celestial music and impossible creatures. It happens to me from time to time and I am sure the same type of metaphor appeals to many a researcher and physicist who most often are philosophers in disguise.

Looking at the ocean, we determine the horizon by the line where the sky meets the ocean. It is not a real line, nor a real limit; it is OUR limit of understanding.

It is what our brain interprets of the sensory input from our eyes. Clearly we know that beyond this line, there is another continent far away; math and physics have long ago proven it through discovery and technology. But it's up to our brain to interpret what we see. This is not always a good thing because we use our brain in a very limited way that is constricted by our perceptions from our first five senses. It's a good start however, and an efficient way of staying alive on a classical physics level but it is not very productive at grasping other scales of magnitude. For these scales, we can rely only on the mathematical abstractions, which do not offer humanly attractive interpretations. For over a hundred years, theoretical physicists such as Werner Heisenberg have stated that language is incapable of describing the fundamental concepts of subatomic reality. According to them, such understandings can only come from metaphor and mental images.

Catherine Pepin, a French theoretical physicist, says, "There are three horizons of perception in physics: relativity for cosmically large systems, quantum mechanics for the infinitesimally small and consciousness where the human brain interprets the information and data spread out in the universe."

No matter any which way we take science, it all comes down to our interpretations of equations and formulas. We humans have to explain what mathematics is saying. And sometimes it can be confusing and very paradoxical.

Our problem? The two horizons of perception of the infinitely big and the infinitesimally small can't seem to reconcile themselves into one big theory of everything as it seems that what works on a cosmic scale does not at a subatomic level and vice versa. However, one sure thing is that both horizons have one thing in common! We humans make the interpretation of the observations. The mathematics, the data, the information-theoretic existence of both horizons is filtered by our brain. That leads to two results: 1) We create a third horizon of perception. Both the quantum and the cosmic scales exist in their own reference frames and are interpreted in a third reference frame, namely the human brain. 2) If the physics of the very small does not reconcile with the physics of the very big it might just be because our brain does not have the capability to do it, or that we do not use our full intellectual capacities to solve it.

To go back to the subject of consciousness, it is important to first understand the foundation of all the physical and mathematical theories of space and time and the relation they have with the way we interpret them.

Of all the actual quantum and cosmic theories, only two account for consciousness.

Some theories look at time as a linear object which leads back to a singularity at the beginning, and thus generates the "why" and "what was before that?" type problems; while other theories conceive of time as a looping concept which would allow no beginning and no end. This solves the Singularity issue but does not answer the "Why does the universe exist?", as it would appear to have created itself. Finally, some others picture the universe as a finite object where all time and space occur all at once without any cause and effect. This theory, favored by many theoretical physicists, considers time and space to be functions of interpretation by the human brain but not fundamental properties of the universe. It does not really give a reason for the creation of the universe but answers in a very compelling way our questions about death and dying! If all time and all space are already created, then time is no longer linear and our life or our death can no longer be considered chronological events but must be acknowledged as unique instances, accessible at any given time and in any place. This is one of the main reasons why this book is being written and we will come back to it in further chapters.

In fact, as we will see, the truth lies in the alchemy of all these interpretations.

Let's explore a few models.

The "no boundary" model
At our classical level, reality is made of three spatial dimensions and a fourth dimension of linear time. This is what we call a Euclidian space. You all have experienced the Euclidian space at school when you were learning geometry or Newtonian classic mechanics. At different scales, such as cosmic scales or subatomic levels, the same Euclidian space can't be used to explain the behavior of things.

In 1908, Hermann Minkowski, Einstein's teacher, was the first one to introduce a revolutionary idea: space and time should be joint together in a continuum called "space-time". This new imaginary dimension is not linear as it heeds space-time's distortions. (Imaginary time is not something made up like unreal time; imaginary time is to time as imaginary numbers are to real numbers.)

In the **No Boundary Model**, the universe has been expanding from the Big Bang on a linear time line and presents itself like a cone of expansion. (Fig 1)

According to this model favored by Stephen Hawking (and Hartle), there is no need for an outside God to create the Singularity if we consider an imaginary time in which both Singularity and space-time exist. The Singularity becomes just a smooth point in that space-time – imaginary time universe.

So, although while human-perceived time might think there is a Big Bang boundary, according to this theory, imaginary time transcends ordinary time and there is in fact no boundary between the universe before and after the Big Bang. This "no boundary" theory states that the laws of physics always apply to the universe. The universe never was a single point of infinite mass, but rather expanded by new creation of the universe from pre-existing energy. This theory states that space-time (imaginary time) always has existed and pre-existed the material universe. Even Stephen Hawkins, in his lectures on this, admits that this is very hard to conceptualize or explain as it is a mathematical concept that does not translate well into language.

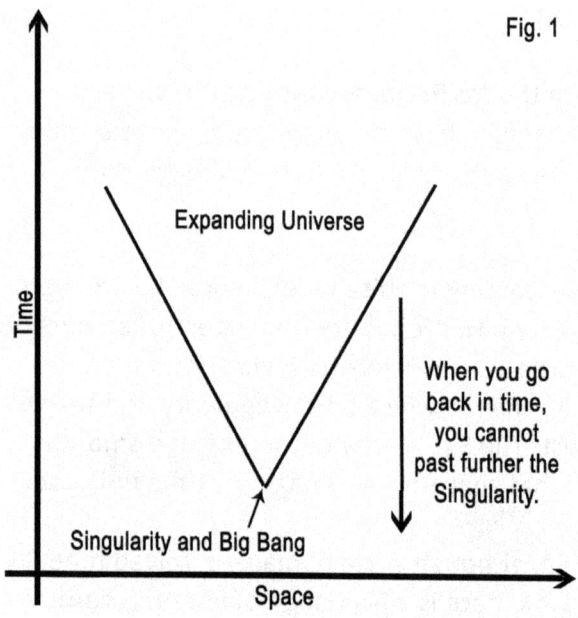

Fig. 1

So, to consider the universe in an imaginary time, mathematicians operate a rotation of the time axis of 90° counterclockwise. In mathematical terms, it is called a "wick rotation" (defined in the next paragraph); the time axis is converted to a complex number and is now the imaginary time axis. (Fig 2)

Wick Rotation

Fig 2

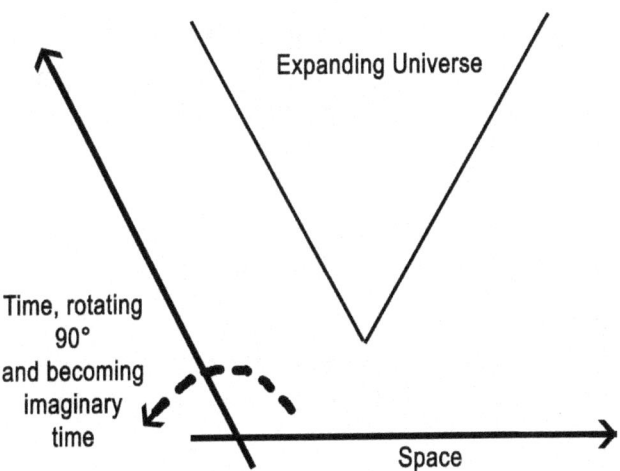

Applying a wick rotation is basically trying to find a solution to a similar or related problem from one space to another. (in mathematical terms again, we are now looking at the universe in this new space called Minkowski space vs the traditional Euclidean space.) Then each point of the function is re-evaluated as a space-time event in a four-dimensional space where time is again a real dimension (vs imaginary).

To do this, mathematicians repeat the rotation but 90° clockwise this time, the imaginary time axis is now pointing upward and downward and allows us to look at the universe with a different view, (new eyes!) (Fig 3).

By doing so, we see how the point of origin, the singularity, disappears (it's all in the math!) and reveals a no boundary space-time curved universe. This might seem a little strange if we do not have the mathematical knowledge to compute it (I don't have it, by the way), but trusting mathematics helps us grasp concepts.

Yet, I am going to try to describe this rotation with a metaphor (which will not be correct

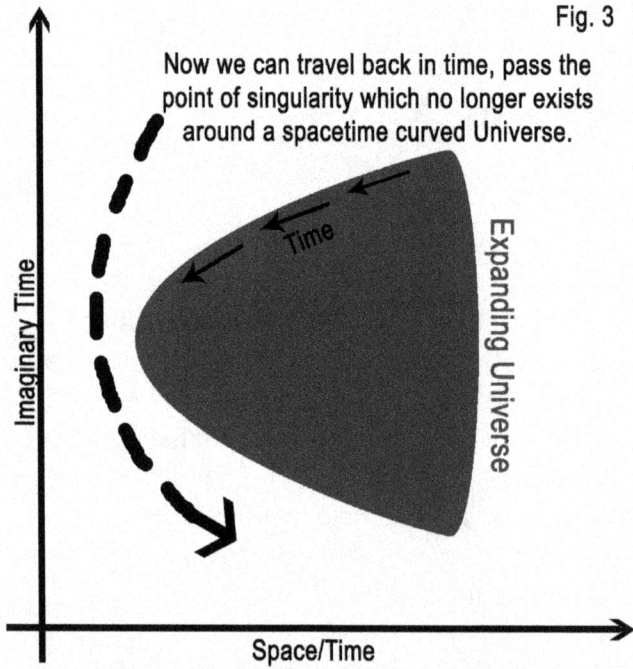

Fig. 3

mathematically this time): It's a bit like doing a load of laundry. If you have a top-loading machine, once you put the laundry in it and you start the machine, you can't see the bottom anymore. You can't even get close to the bottom, nor see beyond it, as the machine is standing upright on the ground. But then imagine, you can rotate your machine into a front-loading position; the original bottom of the washing tub is now in an accessible position. You can virtually walk around your washing machine and around what was the "bottom" of the tub before (the Singularity). Besides from the front-loading glass you can actually see horizontally where the "old bottom of the tub" is, yet it's no longer a "bottom" (a Singularity), it is not a sticking point anymore. Yet, your load of laundry hasn't changed one bit, it is the same load, that will be washed the same way. Sometimes, just applying a rotation can help view things in a new light.

Once again, what happens from this point is how we interpret the mathematical equations, what we understand from these types of diagrams.

In these diagrams, it is easy to see that the singularity is no longer a point of beginning but just a turning point into a curved time universe model. When we go back in time, we curve around; there is no "before the Big Bang" issue anymore because there is no time before the creation of the universe. Time is self-contained in the universe. We see the universe from a new frame of reference.

That also solves the "Why", there is no need for a why. The universe just exists, it is, at least it does mathematically. So, we now have a model in which the universe does not need a God to exist and we have causality of a sort, but not the direct linear cause and effect causality that we perceive as filtered through the human brain.

However, does this mathematical universe satisfy the human heart? Is this fundamentally a fulfilling theory? In this model, is consciousness even relevant? If everything existed in the universe, the galaxies, planets, time, we humans, without any reason to be, why are we always running after the answer to the "Why"?

If all sentient beings and things in the whole wide universe did not exist, would there be no awareness of existence? Is the universe self-aware? So many questions we will attempt to tackle in the following chapters.

The Participatory universe – "It from Bit"
John Archibald Wheeler, Professor Emeritus at Princeton University and the man behind the H-Bomb, among other achievements, proposed another type of universe. In his model, consciousness and information are key to its existence.

John Wheeler stated that the material universe with all its physical laws is dependent on observations by the human mind. This makes the universe very much a participatory universe with consciousness being an active part in creating our perception of material reality. Though Wheeler was fundamentally against parapsychology and psi research being named a science, his very own theory permits the existence of psi phenomena including extra sensory perception, psychic mediumship, Controlled Remote Viewing, and Spiritual Sight among other things. John Wheeler proposed that material reality can be represented by bits of information, which have at their basis an immaterial "bottom" or source. Such an immaterial source was not well defined by Wheeler but certainly could be understood as consciousness. Wheeler speculated that reality is in fact created by human observers of the universe.

He has toyed with the perennial philosophical paradox of human kind in which the very fact of being human and manifesting the universe's reality through our brain, goes directly against our own current scientific understandings that we are an insignificant quantum of the universe within that same universe.

He wrote:

"The brain is small. The universe is large. In what way, if any, is it, the observed, affected by man, the observer? Is the universe deprived of all meaningful existence in the absence of mind? Is it governed in its structure by the requirement that it gives birth to life and consciousness? Or is man merely an unimportant speck of dust in a remote corner of space? In brief, are life and mind irrelevant to the structure of the universe – or are they central to it?" (J.A.Wheeler 1975)"

For Wheeler, we exist in a participatory universe. Coining the term "it from bit" in 1990, he went on to describe that everything, all the matter and all the energy of the universe is information-theoretic derived. (Everything comes from a bit, a bit being the smallest information quantity in a binary system, 1 or 0.) In other words, everything in the universe is the result of a "Yes" or "No" answer to very simplistic binary questions.

In his model, the reality of everything in the universe arises from the binary answers retrievable by the brains of sentient beings and their analyzing apparatuses, such as the ones used in experimental quantum physics. Simply put, consciousness creates the universe in a quantum way. In addition, and this is a "bonus" of this model, it does not matter that the observers can create past events, as in this proposal the universe exists because we are aware of it. (Fig 4)

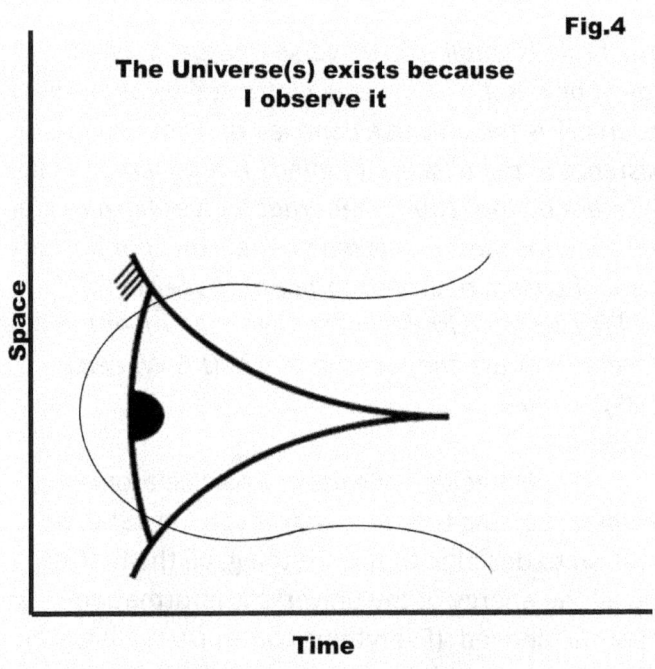

Fig.4
The Universe(s) exists because I observe it

In this very tempting teleological model (where the universe exists because we conceive it and we are part of it ourselves), the human interpretation and awareness are at the forefront of everything. I have to say; this has been one of my preferred ideas for a long time. However, in my peregrination through learning about relativity, quantum mechanics, and cosmology, I realized that this model would not satisfy a few things.

For one, there is no beginning, no end and no causality in this model. Secondly, and most importantly, it postulates that consciousness is linked to us, living observers. This means consciousness is not an intrinsic part of the universe in light of modern consciousness research. I do feel that although Wheeler's model is partially true in the sense that the material universe is information based, "it from bit"; I feel the role and the definition of consciousness are different than the ones described by Wheeler over 50 years ago.

The next model of the universe is given to us by **John Richard Gott** with his **causal loop universe**. According to this model, the universe is self-creating like a systematic time machine. Several Hollywood blockbusters drew inspiration from this model such as Terminator and Back to the Future.

In both movies, an individual (or a robot) is sent back to the past to create or change the future. In the case of Back to the Future, Marty McFly goes to the past to help his future dad and mom to meet otherwise his own existence will be wiped out of the course of time. The causal loop is even better demonstrated when Marty gets stuck in the past and needs his friend Dr. Emmet Brown's invention (The Flux Capacitor) to come back to the future. The trouble is that Dr. Brown hasn't invented it yet; the invention is in the future. Marty however knows about it and plants the idea in Doc's head for him to create it. He can then go back to the future. So, the present depends on the past but the past depends on the future!

One might think that Richard Gott's model of the universe is quite far-fetched. Yet, Richard Gott is no screenwriter nor is he a famous Hollywood director. He is, in fact, a professor of astrophysical science at the very prestigious University of Princeton!

In his model, an advanced civilization could send a probe into the past to ensure its very own creation in the future (Fig. 5).

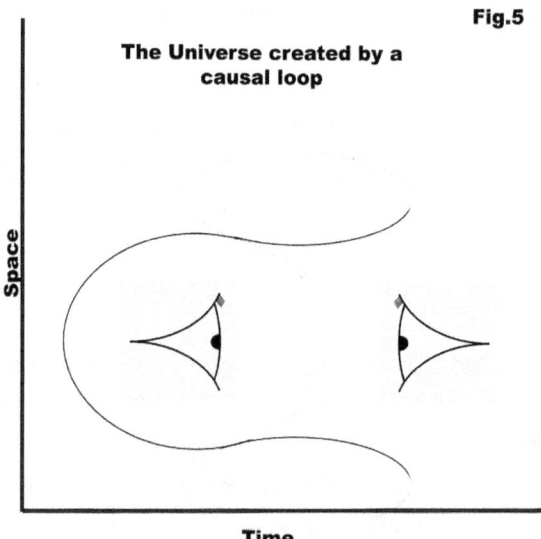

Fig.5

The Universe created by a causal loop

The trouble with that is that it would require human intervention, or at the very least some sort of deliberate act of creation from sentient beings. The universe could create itself over and over again, even creating baby universes.

All this would explain, or rather avoid, the point of Singularity. In this model, there would be many potential universes so the existence of one does not depend on the sudden appearance of the Big Bang. The universe would be endlessly creating itself over and over again in a causal loop.

Our next two candidates are the Wheeler-DeWitt quantum gravity theory and the Hidden Variable Theory. Because both theories are derived from quantum mechanics principles we will tackle these models in the next chapter, where I will discuss quantum theory.

Chapter 5
LET'S EXPLORE THE WHY
PART 2 – QUANTUM MECHANICS AND US

"All the wonders of quantum physics were learned basically from looking at atom-smasher technology. But let me let you in on a secret: We physicists are not driven to do this because of better color television. That's a spin-off. We do this because we want to understand our role and our place in the universe."
— Michio Kaku

Quantum mechanics is the branch of physics that researches and explains the behavior of the infinitesimally small (atoms, particles).

Quantum mechanics, as does its big sister general relativity for large cosmic scales, has a set of wonderful laws and principles that govern the subatomic level; seven to be exact. These seven laws and principles give us insights on how the fundamental building blocks of our universe behave; or at least what we infer from them. Once again, these laws and principles are the derived interpretations of a set of equations, themselves determined by both observations and postulates. In other words, there is the mathematics and then there is what WE make of it.

These principles and laws are utterly fascinating, even if sometimes they seem to denote more science fiction than real science; and in many ways, are toying with pure theoretical concepts that are extremely difficult to grasp and are for the most part counter intuitive to what we can observe and feel at our classical physics human level.

Nevertheless, they are working principles and laws. They carry the hope that one day, with the advent of promising theories such as the String Theory, or Quantum Gravity Theory, they will unify with General Relativity and give us a true and unique picture of our universe. Some of these principles combined together might even help fathom the very beginning of our universe.

To better understand the two models of the universe that will be described in this chapter, let's first review these seven laws and principles of quantum mechanics to familiarize ourselves with their particularities:

1- Superposition (Schrödinger equation)
When we study the movement, position and energy of things in our classical physics level we can calculate the velocity, the position and the energy of these things by deduction. Each calculation gives an image of the state in which things are. Take a golf ball being swung by a golfer: we know how to calculate its position on its trajectory and its velocity based on its original position before the swing and the time spent to reach the position we are measuring at. The ball obeys the laws of classical physics.

In quantum mechanics, a particle can be in a multitude of states at the same time. And until you actually make a measurement to find it in one state or another, there is no objective way to precisely know or deduce what a measurement of a state of that particle will yield in advance. There is no way to infer from previous observations what the results will be like in classical physics (Cartesian reasoning). You have to take a large number of measurements to be able to eventually obtain a measurement of each state of a particle. What quantum mechanics does is that it gives a probability that a particle will be in one state or another. *(We will see this in our point 2, 'inderminism of measurement'.)*

For example, a particle could have two different speeds at the same time, or be in two or more places at the same time! Imagine the golf ball being swung and being idle at the same time, or doing a hole in one but yet missing the hole completely. What a mess! And it remains like this as long as you do not observe the golf ball.

Physicist Erwin Schrodinger comes up with the equation (carrying his name) that clearly demonstrates this paradox. To explain it he creates a virtual experiment, a thought experiment, with a virtual cat in a virtual box. In this apparatus, a deadly poison is to be released when radioactive material randomly emits radiation. His experiment shows that the cat is potentially alive and potentially dead at the same time in the box as long as no one opens it to make an observation: it's the infamous Schrodinger's cat experiment. When the box is open only one outcome can be observed: the cat being dead or the cat being alive. In mathematical terms, when we open the box, we "collapse the equation" into one possible outcome, where the equation itself represents all the possible outcomes for that specific experiment.

All other laws of quantum mechanics derive from this principle.

2- The indeterminism of measurement

We now know a particle exists in many different states at once until it is observed. Each time a single observation is made, a single state is observed and measured. The cumulative results of many measurements yield many outcomes and offer then a statistical probability of the state of a given particle.

So, what do we do to find out the position of an electron for example? Well, instead of considering the electron as a physical particle we start looking at its behavior and if we observe it long enough bouncing off all over at different levels of energy, we start seeing patterns of movement. We can see where the particle has been the most or the least. It creates thus a coefficient of probability of state.

One of the greatest discoveries of quantum mechanics is the realization that nature is not purely deterministic. (i.e. if you know a state of something you cannot logically determine its other states – the opposite of what Descartes affirmed in his Discourse of the Method). Determinism is not an applicable concept at the subatomic level the way it is at the classical (macro) level.

3- The duality wave/particle

Now that we have established the indeterminism of the quantum world and that we have been observing our particle bouncing off all over, we have noticed a pattern.

Let's say our electron is bouncing up and down and is measured 3 times at level 1, 4 times at level 2, 6 times at level 3 and none at level zero. Each state level that the electron is found at has now a coefficient of presence: 3 times here, 4 times there, etc. If we place these coefficients of state onto a graph we can actually see the probability of our electron to be more at level 3 than at level 2 for example. What we obtain is a measurement that looks like one of a wave, like an electromagnetic wave, which actually fluctuates with time. Our particle, which has been bobbing all over, acts like a wave over time; hence it's duality. The duality is not so that a particle switches from being matter to just energy, it is that its behavior is one of a particle but also one of a wave.

The duality is at the center stage of physicists' interrogation about our universe.

However, a recent classical physics experiment has come to challenge the thought that quantum mechanics and classical physics play by two completely different sets of rules. A French physicist, Yves Couder, devised an experiment with a droplet of silicon placed on a vibrating substrate. In this experiment, not only is it revealed that the droplet seems to bounce and never sink in the substrate but it shows that the droplet is carried around by a combination of the waves created by the shake and the bounce onto a "pilot wave". The droplet this way carried, moves around the substrate, in what seems to be a completely random way, transported by its pilot wave. The experiment climaxes when after filming the droplet bouncing around for hours, even days (as the system is very stable), a pattern appears in the droplets movement. That pattern and the droplet/wave behavior are highly analogous to the behavior of a particle/wave combination in the quantum world.

This is very exciting! Could it potentially open a pathway between the two physics (classic – objects at our scale, and quantic – objects at the subatomic level)? More needs to be done obviously but It could at least revive one of the very first theories which attempted to find determinism in the quantum world: The theory of the pilot wave first formulated by French physicist Pf. Louis de Broglie in 1927 and which had been highly criticized by his contemporaries at the time. We will come back to this theory when we address the hidden variables subject later in this chapter.

4- The Uncertainty Principle of Heisenberg
One of the most famous principles of quantum mechanics is Heisenberg's principle of uncertainty. In the first law that we described (the principle of superposition of Schrodinger), we exposed the non-deterministic nature of measurement of a particle.

Now, say we want to measure the position of a particle and its momentum; once we make an observation of its position, the act of observing that particle puts the system in a given state. If we want to immediately measure its momentum it will yield a different result than if we had started to measure its momentum first, before we measured its position. This is because these two observables are incompatible and do not share a full set of states (indeterminism). The uncertainty principle brings to light the limit of precision with which we can simultaneously measure different incompatible observables.

Imagine you are watching a movie of a running cheetah chasing a gazelle at full speed. You can see the cheetah's speed from watching the movie but you can't see where the cheetah is in reference to the background because it is all blurred "by the speed". To be able to see where the cheetah is in reference to the background at a precise time t, you would have to stop the movie and get a single image with no blur in the background, still beaming light on the film. In reality once you have recorded the blurred background, you are stuck with it, but if you could freeze the image in real time, the blur would disappear as soon as you stop the action. You would freeze a frame in time and that frame would give you the exact position of the cheetah in your movie and in reference to the background, but you would lose the ability to measure his speed! To get a measurement of the speed, you'd have to restart the movie (and lose the initial position immediately and your ability to measure it) or you would need to measure its speed first, if you could rewind, (before you measure the position); but then you would find a different measurement of its position as soon as you freeze the frame (and vice versa). And to realize these measurements, and "see" your cheetah's observables, you would have to project a type of light that would be so energetic, that the simple action of observing the feline would influence its own energy, and would blind it and push it off course, which would also influence the measurement!

For particles, it is the same; if you measure their position, the simultaneous measurement of their momentum yields imprecise results (and vice versa). In the quantum world, it is a little more complicated of course than this classical physics thought example because we are dealing with waves and frequencies or levels of energy but the idea is the same.

If we push the analogy of the blurred background, we easily understand that the trouble with the blur does not come from the background itself, or the speed of our cheetah, but from the observer who/which cannot adjust his/its eyes to see clearly both background and the moving target.

The background does not turn "blurry" with speed. Our eyes and the eyes of our physical apparatuses cannot adjust, register and analyze the image, thus they create a blurry, imprecise image.

It is in fact a matter of focus. Which do we choose to focus on? Speed, position or trajectory? This idea of focus will become important when again we tackle all these concepts from a metaphysical point of view.

5- Quantum Tunneling

A direct consequence of the uncertainty principle and the duality wave/particle comes in the form of quantum tunneling. In many ways, the quantum world is the dream world for ghost hunters. We have *"spooky actions at a distance"* as Einstein would describe it, ubiquity capabilities with the principles of superposition and uncertainty and now walking through walls!

Quantum tunneling is a phenomenon that allows a particle-wave to go through a barrier.

Let's go back to our golf ball. The golfer swings the club and hits the ball. Bad move, it's headed to the clubhouse wall. No panic, no Problem! As the ball hits the wall, some of it bounces back on to the green but the rest goes through the wall and lands in a hole in one on the other side! Part of the ball tunneled through the wall!

How about this for a crazy story? Of course, at our classical level, this does not really happen, but deep at the subatomic level, because particles behave like waves, it is a reality. When they hit a barrier, like a sound wave hits a wall, some of that wave, with a reduced amplitude due to the impact, goes through the barrier.

To use the analogy of the sound, it is easy to imagine your neighbor's too loud music that goes through the walls and makes its way into your bedroom, muffled but still audible and ruining your night. It is the same with subatomic particles, these little specs of matter. Then a question arises. "Is it the particle which really goes through the wall or is it its wave property?"

In other words, is it the massive particle that makes it through the wall or is it the information, the properties of the particles, which have no barrier. This is a question that we will also tackle in a metaphysical way later.

6- Path Integral formulation – double slit experiment

Another experiment that is quite famous in quantum mechanics is the Double Slit Experiment of Thomas Young, an English scientist from the 19th century. Originally the experiment had been created to show the wave property of light, but then was applied to other particles such as electrons.

This experiment demonstrated the wave-particle duality and suggested that a quantum particle does not necessary have one trajectory, but several at the same time. Building upon the previous work of Paul Dirac, one of the fathers of quantum mechanics and contemporary of Schrodinger, Richard Feynman discovers in 1948 the way to calculate and formulate a functional integral of all possible trajectories of a particle from a point A to a point B, in the form of a quantum wave amplitude.

In the double slit experiment, a beam of electrons is projected through a single slit first, then two slits. The electrons are projected either as a beam or one by one. Each time, an observation is made on a screen where the electrons hit, as well as at the slit(s), where the electrons pass through.

Not only has this experiment demonstrated the wave function of a particle as the electron projected acts like a wave going through both slits at the same time but it also has enabled calculation of the probabilities of finding the electron imprint on the screen based on all the possible routes the electron could take (through one slit, two, one or the other).

As a side note, this experiment also showed that an observer can only measure one state of a particle at a time while that same particle continues to exist in other states. (New revolutionary science in quantum computers however, has now been able to build and measure a Qubit, a two state – at the same time - mechanical system. This exponentially increases the speed of processing information. Qubit, or quantum bit, is the quantum equivalent of the classical bit (the smallest measurement of information of binary type)). This will be discussed further in a later chapter.

7- Quantization
We now know that particles can be observed and measured as probabilities of wave amplitude. If we consider these quantic waves as ripples on water, each undulation of the wave, each level of that undulation, is characterized by a certain level of energy that can be realistically measured. Each level of energy of our particle is characterized by a quantum of energy, within the field of energetic amplitude of that specific particle.

Each particle has a very specific energy quantum at different levels (a reason why, for example, electrons orbit around the nucleus and don't come crashing into it).

When there is no quantum to be measured in a field, it is called a quantum vacuum. This is how and why quantum mechanics got its name!

Does a quantum vacuum mean that there is nothing there or just nothing to be measured? Another question we will tackle later, when we describe the creation of the universe with the hidden variables and inflation theories that we promised you in chapter 4. All these laws and principles have borne many an interpretation since the beginning of quantum mechanics.

One of the first interpretations to be fathomed was the Copenhagen Interpretation, formulated by Niels Bohr and Werner Heisenberg. In this interpretation, the duality of particles is only measurable as a discontinuous, non-causal series of probabilities of one state or another. In other words, the quantum world would be characterized by its indeterminism unlike the determinism of nature and the universe at larger scale. This interpretation has led the race over all the other interpretations for many years, since it was first articulated in the late 1920s, and has found few challengers to threaten its legacy. However, in recent years two new ideas have imposed themselves: The Many World Interpretation (The Everett interpretation) with the notion of decoherence and the Hidden Variable Theory (theory of De Broglie and Bohm). We will talk about hidden variables and decoherence further down in this chapter.

Now before going back to our original quest to understand the origin of the universe and the last two theories based on quantum mechanics, we have to make a very quick stop by the concept of the forces that hold our universe together.

The universe is composed of four fundamental forces: gravity which is the curvature of space-time and holds you down on Earth, electromagnetism which makes the atoms stick together – that's why you are not falling through your chair - the strong nucleus force which holds the elementary particles of the atom's nucleus together, and the weak nucleus force which is the radioactive decay of particles provoked by the emission or the absorption of sub-particles. The radioactive decay allows the constant creation and recycling of new particles.

One would think that these four main forces should work at every level on the different scales of the universe, small or big. The problem is they don't; more precisely, gravity does not.

Gravity is the troublemaker at the subatomic level. Gravity at very small levels cannot be made small itself. One of the two main theories that try to reconcile the large scales and the subatomic level is the theory of Quantum Gravity (the other one is Superstring theory). In the Quantum Gravity theory, gravity, which is a property of space-time, is quantized in an almost infinite and discontinued number of quanta instead of being measured functionally based on a continuous time. This theory may be tested both at a quantum level and an astronomical level. Superstring Theory, which depicts every single sub particle as little vibrating strings has been a great contender for the unification of the four forces of our universe. However, it is very difficult considering the scale at which these strings operate to test the theory; this is why it hasn't been as successful as anticipated since its first conception in 1943 by Werner Heisenberg and its revival as superstring theory in the 80's.

This brings us to our two last versions of the creation and reason of the existence of our universe:

The **Wheeler-DeWitt quantum gravity theory**, as we briefly saw, attempts to reconcile the large and small scales, to provide a concise picture of the universe, its creation and evolution.

To understand the problem and the solution offered by the Wheeler-DeWitt model, one has to understand what quantum mechanics does, what general relativity does and what quantum gravity is trying to do.

Quantum mechanics as we saw previously in this chapter, is the theory that explains the behavior of particles interacting and moving within the universe and its space-time intrinsic nature; general relativity is the theory that explains how large objects interact and move within the universe when placed in the gravitational space-time essence of the universe. Quantum gravity attempts to explain the behavior of gravity within the space-time continuum itself, as a quantum field. It aims at quantizing gravity by quantizing space and time themselves; *"that is by considering elementary units of time and elementary units of space, or even atoms of time and atoms of space. The entire universe then becomes a discontinuous fabric made of grains of space"*. That's what the French astrophysicist, Jean-Pierre Luminet, research director at the CNRS (National Center for Scientific Research) says.

The resultant of the Wheeler-DeWitt equation of quantization of gravity shows that the rate of change of state of the universe with respect to time is zero. In another words the universe does not change with time because time and space are all spread out.

It sounds like a nonsensical statement when we see things change all the time, as humans on our planet, observing the universe from within!

But the answer is right here. We are WITHIN the universe; we are ONE with it. However, for a hypothetical outside observer, the universe is a whole including space, time and us. There is no frame of reference outside it; thus, no way of knowing where the universe is or how old it is and where it is coming from. The time and space contained in the universe do not exist outside of it.

Subsequently, we can only measure an object inside the universe's reference frame. There is no clock outside the universe and time and space are spread out entirely within the universe. There is no observer outside the universe. There is no absolute frame of reference outside the universe. See Fig 6a and 6b.

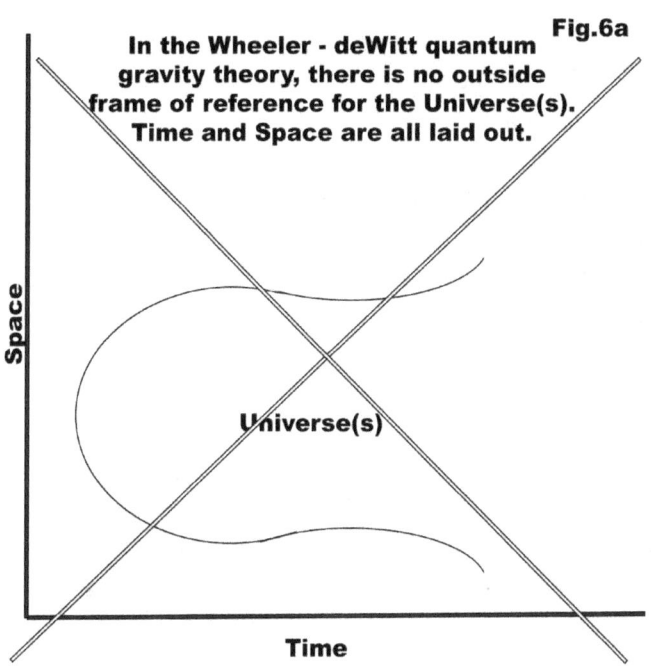

Fig.6a

In the Wheeler - deWitt quantum gravity theory, there is no outside frame of reference for the Universe(s). Time and Space are all laid out.

Fig.6b

Instead, Time and Space are contained inside the Universe(s) and everything within is relative to everything else. Yet the Universe(s) itself has no reference of Space/Time existence outside of it.

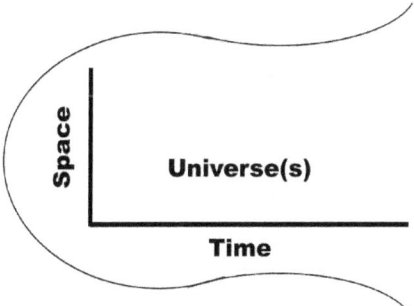

Now, since space and time are all spread out, there is no point that is more real than another one! From a hypothetical outside point of view, every single point in the universe is indistinct from the next, thus there is no past, no present, and no future. Time is only a human perception or as Einstein liked to call it: *"An illusion"*.

For the point of view that interests us, "mortal" beings, the beauty of this model is that, because all is spread out, our death is just a point in that particular universe among many other points representing us alive in that same universe. An outside observer would be able to see us dead and alive at the same time. The point of our death relative to time is only the resultant of our interpretation of time within the universe.

Reality is nothing but a magic trick; you have to look at it from a different angle to see what's really going on. One of these illusions that we are going to discuss presents itself in the form of the **"Hidden Variable Theory"**.

Quantum mechanics lays its foundation on the principle of uncertainty. In quantum mechanics, we constantly have an imprecise measurement. Indeed, when we focus on a specific measurement of a state of a particle all the other measurable quantities do not seem to be available to us. These other quantities are called hidden variables. Because of these hidden variables it is impossible to have a complete true picture of our world at the subatomic level.

What some physicists have concluded is that quantum mechanics is incomplete and does not suffice to describe an entire system. There must be another complete theory that would avoid indeterminism in the measurement and thus give a clear description of a system at any given time.

Einstein was one of the most fervent opponents to the indeterminism of quantum mechanics and summarized his view when he said, "*God does not play dice*".

Two theories then appeared. The first one is a re-emergence of a once forgotten and refuted theory formulated by the father of quantum mechanics, Pf. Louis De Broglie. The theory, revisited by physicist David Bohm in 1952, postulates that each particle (which presents the duality wave-particle) would actually be guided by a pilot wave and that the intrinsic link between the pilot wave and the particle would solve the indeterminism in the measure as both would be linked and measurable at the same time.

The pilot wave theory induces realism and determinism. What we see is real and not the product of interpretation by an observer. In Chapter five we talked about a classical physics experiment created in 2010 by Pr. Yves Couder at the University of Diderot in Paris using droplets of silicon oil on a substrate of silicon shaken to a certain frequency. Pr. Couder discovered that not only do the droplets of silicon act like a subatomic particle bouncing around in an apparent probabilistic way, but also that the frequencies of the shaking table interfering with the waves, made by the bouncing droplet, created a pilot wave by which the droplet was actually guided throughout its bouncing around the table; illustrating at the classical physics level the once denied De Broglie theory and thus reopening its candidacy to quantum mechanics Hidden Variables Determinism Theory.

In the Hidden Variable Theory, physicists postulate that below the ground of quantum mechanics there is a hidden level, a secret level. At the deepest level of quantum mechanics, where there is nothing, there is something. That something can be measured by a wave function (as we know everything as a duality of wave-particle). This ground zero is the quantum vacuum. Yet, this quantum vacuum is far from being empty.

If we consider the origin of the universe (and our mortal position within it), which has been our main quest in these last two chapters, it's hard to believe that things appeared out of nothingness. Once again, as humans we have the need to find a causality for everything.

French physicist, Bernard d'Espagnat, professor emeritus at the University of Orsay Paris Sud, suggests a solution by postulating the existence of an underlying layer that he calls veiled reality. Elementary particles emerge and disappear constantly from this layer. Our problem is not the legitimacy of the existence of this veiled reality, but our inability to detect it and to see it.

Austro-Americano Physicist Fritjof Capra says: "[...] *Subatomic particles are not static and permanent, but dynamic and transitory, coming into being and vanishing in one ceaseless dance of movement and energy. [...] According to field theory, the vacuum is far from empty. On the contrary, it contains an unlimited number of particles which come into being and vanishing without end [...]*" - The Tao of Physics

What the Hidden Variable Theory teaches us is that by knowing all layers and all levels of energies of all the particles, we would then be able to use determinism to explain and understand our universe, the same way we use it in classical physics, at our human level. Subsequently, we would have the answers to all our existential questions concerning the beginning of our universe.

Again, because of the scale of these particles, and the minute life span they have, it is very difficult to test this theory. CERN (The European Organization for Nuclear Research) in Switzerland, with its famous atom collider, has been quite successful though, in unraveling bits and pieces of this secret layer, and there is much hope that it can continue giving us a better understanding of our quantum world in the years to come.

Another theory, which tends to give credit to this hidden variable veiled reality layer is **the Many World Theory (The Everett Interpretation).** It uses an explanatory mechanism called decoherence.

The Many World Theory was formulated by Hugh Everett in 1957 and has been revisited by several scientists since then, including cosmologist Max Tegmark, author of "Our Mathematical universe".

In one of his papers "The Interpretation of Quantum Mechanics: Many World or Many Words?", Max Tegmark puts the Many World theory to the test of our human interpretation and aims at finding a real fundament to its claim comparing it to other interpretations. He concludes that it's all a matter of trusting mathematical language vs human language.

In quantum mechanics, there are two fundamental ways to look at an experiment: The mathematical way, which will look at the wave function evolution of a particle and will have causality by having an *Outside View,* envisioning all possible outcomes; and the observer way in which the observer will be caught into an *Inside View* of the system he is observing, collapsing the wave function into one and only possible outcome at a time.

However, there is a beautiful event that comes to the rescue of the observer and could potentially be the gateway into this hidden variables' secret: It's called decoherence.

Decoherence is the time window during which one could potentially observe a system interact with its surroundings, still in a superposed state. This window is usually very short: 10^{-30} second! During that time period the system oscillates between its different possible states based on its energy interaction with its surrounding. These oscillations are called Rabi oscillations. They show that in its indeterministic state, a system could still offer an incredible view of all its possible outcomes at the same time based on its interaction with its surroundings. That is a phenomenal window into the potential explanation of space and time being all spread out since the beginning of the universe and even the state of the universe at its very beginning.

Decoherence is probably one of the most coherent mechanisms observed at the subatomic level, allowing the observer to have a very short but yet compelling "outside view" of the everything-ness of a system.

After reviewing all these scientific notions, what can we infer about consciousness? The second part of this book is going to actually tackle the subject. Is consciousness all spread out like time and space? Does it act like an outside viewer trying all possible solutions? Or is it "*an emergent phenomenon like wetness or solidity*?" as theoretical physicist Sean Caroll once answered me in one of his live Facebook chats.

Chapter 6
OH, MY GOD!

"It may seem bizarre, but in my opinion science offers a surer path to God than religion."
–Physicist Paul Davies,

Now that we have reviewed the main theories that attempt to explain our universe in its infinitesimally small and big scales and we have looked at some of these theories as potential ways to unravel the mysteries of our existence, one legitimate question is, "Do any of these theories really answer the 'why' question?"

Where do we stand? Do these theories even start to shed light on our human condition, on our self-awareness and on our consciousness? Do they contribute to our understanding of the existence of God? Do they give us the assurance of the continuity of our life?

As a scientific medium, I have long thought that we humans have created God as a reflection of ourselves to feel protected and to fill the void caused by the uncertainty of our existence; an emptiness we have felt since the dawn of humanity. This void is created by our lack of perspective and our lack of global vision. Our very presence within the universe induces the idea that there is something greater than us that rules everything. Yet we must be careful to not project our fears and anxieties on the universe and in doing so create the notion of a "God", be it a single creator God or the hundreds of gods worshipped by early humans, each corresponding to a particular fear or anxiety.

When we came up with the notion of God, in this fashion, we gave God all the attributes of our human condition, we made him (her) all that we ought to be if we were his (her) perfect subjects. Instead of God creating us in her/his image, I am suggesting that we created a god or gods in our image. We gave God credit for our extraordinary resilience, beauty, awareness, and propensity to love. We also gave God the power to destroy us as a species. In doing so, we discarded the responsibility of our own evolution and decisions into the hands of God.

Are we in a participatory universe? Did we create it from nothing including God? Or is God behind the hidden veiled reality, acting like the patron saint of the hidden variables that started it all? If we position ourselves as observers of our own realities, are we not the constant creators of the very God we are so desperately seeking? Who or what is God? And if God created the universe, why did he/she do so?

During his 2015 historical visit to the USA, Pope Francis spoke to the Congress, visited prisons and spoke to inmates, and gave a mass to a packed Madison Square Garden crowd of over eighteen thousand people. As I listened to his different interventions, I was pleasantly surprised to discover the forward-thinking capabilities and attitude of his Holiness.

He is the first pontiff in the history of Christianity who openly regards the questions of science in a logical and agreeable way. What a breath of fresh air! Although most Christians will argue that men of the Church had to study science and mathematics as a part of ascending to their vocation, history shows that if said science contradicted religious doctrines, it would be at best ignored, and at worst vilified; the defenders of science hunted down with death threats. Galileo is one of the most probing examples!

This is why the views of Pope Francis and his actions are commendable.

One thing he said really struck a chord with me. A child came to him and asked, *"Pope Francis, what did God do before he created the world?"*

Perplexed, the pontiff paused a few seconds and then answered the child with these words: *"Before God created the world, God loved. God had so much love, and that love was so great and so overflowing that God could not be egocentric, so that love had to be poured out to be shared. And from that point, God created the world."*

As anecdotal as this beautiful story might seem, I cannot help but draw a parallel between the overflowing love and the need to expand it, and quantum fluctuations creating enough energy to trigger inflation and then the expansion of our universe that we have observed. How exciting that we are part of this expansion, on our tiny planet.

Oh, My God! Did Pope Francis just solve the Religion-Science long-term antagonism with this simple statement to a child? Maybe just a little. My contribution is to point out that religion based on the notion of a loving god and science based on understanding reality as a participatory quantum energy field both refer to the same thing, just using a different language.

One consists of mathematical equations and the other uses the language of allegories. They are not fundamentally different, because the language of mathematics requires interpretations to be understood at our level. God is one interpretation among many others.

William Ockham, a theologian from the 14th century paradoxically came up with a way of determining which theory is the most acceptable when several emerge on the same subject: The Ockham's Razor. Ockham's Razor states that among two or more theories, the one that uses fewer assumptions is the one that most likely will reveal itself as true. It does not dismiss the others, but in the absence of more data, the less guesses, the better.

After reviewing the main theories about the existence of our universe, can we adjudicate one as the true explanation? Of course, not. Scientists are still trying to find that ONE theory of everything (TOE) that will unify all physics. It is normal to struggle with our own choices. However, let's see if we can determine which theory seems to have the least assumptions?

Is there no godly reason for the universe to exist like Stephen Hawkins suggests in his no boundary model? Or are we creating the universe ourselves in a participatory universe? Or is it that the hidden variables of the universe are just love from which everything is created and annihilated until the "love" became so powerful that it acted like an antigravity force and pushed our universe into a tremendous inflation followed by a homogenous expansion?

In the latter question, the assumption is that there is a purposeful God that created everything that we see, hear, feel, touch, smell and more. This would satisfy causality. There must be an outside source that started it all. Would it go against scientific observations? Yes, and no, because in reality, we cannot observe the hidden variables through the hidden veiled reality any more than we can observe God. Yet, they are today admitted as a true viable scientific possibility whereas God, with regards to science, is a figment of man's imagination.

The hidden veiled reality could be called "the hidden veiled reality" or "love" or "God"; its true nature cannot be determined. In fact, it is just a question of semantics. All such names have equal scientific value and justification with regards to causality claims.

Yet, if we accept that our known universe exists with no causality other than a causal feedback loop, it would seem to eliminate the need for God. The no boundary model and the participatory universe just help us understand that our place in the universe is as important as anyone and anything else because there is no reason for us to "be" as there is no reason for the cosmos to "be". "According to this line of thinking, we are the universe and we create the universe".

So, can we apply William Ockham's Razor here? The problem is that we are trying to solve the greatest mystery of all with our human brains, which are beautiful machines, but extremely limited by our human condition on our tiny planet in a rather small galaxy, part of a huge cluster of galaxies, floating somewhere in the expanding universe. Our vantage point of observation is just one point and certainly not the only one nor the true one. Our understanding of reality is only as true as we can interpret it via our senses.

The only true language is mathematics.

On one hand, with mathematics, we are forced to look at things in an abstract way that is stripped of interpretation because mathematics is everywhere. It is in the flower in the garden and in the pulsar in space. It is in the geometry of the inside of a red cabbage and in the distribution of cosmological objects in the universe. Mathematics does not need hidden variables because the quantum wave function works for any state of any particle. Is mathematics "The Holy spirit"? Or would mathematics be more like the universal language of God as chaos mathematicians suggest? Can we compute love in a mathematical formula?

Now, on the other hand, if we associate God with the quantum hidden veiled reality, and we say that God is love, then we are placing a human feeling at the beginning of the universe. By doing so, every single explanation of the universe we attempt to give becomes flawed by our very own human condition. We are still confronted with our original teleological problem in which the apparition of a phenomenon (the universe) is explained by a final cause (thinking humans, beings with feelings, within that same universe).

How do we get out of this mind-boggling loop?

The only plausible explanation would be that the very thing that makes us sentient beings with all our feelings, information and knowledge, aka consciousness, pre-existed the beginning, the hidden variables, or any God.

Consciousness must have come first or at least at the same time than the first quantum fluctuation!

Chapter 7
CONSCIOUSNESS AND THE UNIVERSE(s)

"We are the cosmos made conscious and life is the means by which the universe understands itself."
— Physicist Brian Cox

Billions of years of evolution have transformed our brains into sophisticated machines, incessant seekers of answers to the "why" question.

Once we take away the "why" from the equation though, we can have a healthy relationship with the core of the universe. That same core Nicolai Tesla says exists and holds all knowledge and inspiration. If that core exists, and there is no godly reason for it to be, does it appear out of nothingness?

Science and spirituality are our only tools to understand how the core is functioning. This core could be described as a whole in which time, space and consciousness play a main role in holding all knowledge. Inspired by the hunch that led Minkowski to propose a new unit of space-time, as we saw in our chapter 4, new scientists such as Michio Kaku feel that we can indeed quantify consciousness as dimensional units, or "grains of consciousness". Let's imagine for a second that we combine these three-dimensional units of space, and the 4th dimensional unit of space-time with consciousness units, wouldn't we have an exact positioning of space-time-consciousness for each event that has ever happened

I AM, THEREFORE I THINK

and will happen? From that point, any human brain, any brain of any species or even any machine for that matter, could access this information. (by brain, I also mean the sensors of a photoelectric cell for example).

We have reviewed in our chapter 4, that time and space emerged right at the time of the Big Bang, because the laws of physics did not seem to start working before that moment. Nothing at this point prevents us to postulate that consciousness is not subjected to the same constraint as we have already hinted in previous chapters. It is easy to conceptualize that when the first quantum fluctuation came out in existence, so did the first unit of consciousness. During inflation, consciousness expanded as well. Consciousness was born to allow time and space to do the same.

According to the Wheeler-DeWitt theory we just reviewed in chapter 5, time and space have been spread out entirely within the universe. If consciousness is the global information of the universe, it would be logical that its existence started prior to the hidden veiled reality concept; and if it did, then the information about the hidden variables are only hidden because we can't observe them with our brains or technology, not because the information does not exist or is some sort of magical mystery or unicorn.

Our consciousness horizon of perception is very limited because our brain is limited. Hence it is easier to observe in the present than to remember in the past or foresee the future. As a matter of fact, the very structure of our brain has been created and perfected for millions of years to allow us to follow a time line from past to future. This is how we interpret the time spread out for us in classical physics, within the universe we live; otherwise it would be very confusing and quite paralyzing if we were to perceive everything at once. We would not be able to make any decision as we would have to sort through too much information. In a sense, our body and brain are exactly built to process the right amount of information to keep us sane. The sci-fi movie "Interstellar" depicts this pretty well, when the hero, Matthew McConaughey, finds himself inside a black hole falling into a structure that happens to be his daughter's bedroom through time. The structure contains an almost infinite number of sub-cells, all being his daughter's bedroom at any given time. He has to sort through so much information to find the one cell that is going to be useful for him and ultimately will allow him to communicate through space-time and reach out to his daughter at the right moment to save the world.

In this model, consciousness becomes a concept of information that we interpret through our sensory perceptions and brain. Each brain being unique, each interpretation is unique. Yet, the original information is true in its wholeness, and thus universal. The actual definition of consciousness, in medical terms and in dictionaries, leaves out completely the notion of information to focus entirely on the awareness of a person. I wholeheartedly believe this is wrong. It seems to me that awareness is awareness and consciousness has nothing to do with awareness. If consciousness is indeed a concept of information, someone could have lost awareness and still be very conscious. This occurs, for example, in patients in a coma who are nonetheless conscious of their surroundings; in people who have a near-death experience, which has been shown to occur at the point of death when the person is not aware; or even during sleep, where there clearly is consciousness but not awareness.

Losing awareness is only a state of that person (as being aware is another state of existence of that same person). In quantum mechanics, the complete information of a system is embedded in its wave function and it's only when the wave function collapses that some of the information becomes inaccessible to the observer. But one of the very important facts of our universe, which physicists agree on today, is that whatever happens, even if we theoretically fall into a black hole, which swallows everything, the information of us and of everything is preserved and never disappears. Since we postulate that consciousness is the global information of everything, it must be preserved as a whole, encompassing all the states of a person. An individual person's consciousness is part of the universal consciousness. It is indeed the universal consciousness manifesting in the individual person utilizing that person's brain. Awareness, on the other hand, is specific to a given person and the function of his or her brain.

And as consciousness expands, the information of the "I am" expands with it and is constantly recorded in the dimension of consciousness, like a dot with its own space-time coordinates. Then, the collection of all these dots becomes accessible to our memory. When I turn Descartes' saying on its head and make it "I am, therefore I think", I am postulating a very multi-layered consciousness; the "I am" resonates from many levels throughout the universe.

The incredible beauty of this model is that there would be that very point of information, be it in the past or in the future, that would be accessible, in the continuity of the expansion of our universe. As we are part of the universe, the startling implication of this model is that in theory we have access to every point of information in the universe, past, present or future.

If consciousness exists as a stand-alone phenomenon of the universe, consciousness must create our realities through our senses and must allow instant communication between all the elements of the universe as all is interconnected. Some scholars and academics would argue that this is pure metaphysics that has no ground in science as consciousness is an emerging phenomenon directly linked to the sensation of being aware. Again, I feel that we have to look at consciousness from the point of view of information. If we turn it around from being a human emerging phenomenon to a global and universal information concept it becomes easy to theorize that all information being connected and preserved, it is only our human condition that has such a restricted use of it.

This huge realization comes at a time when humanity is in great need of a spiritual shift as well.

Chapter 8
HOW DOES CONSCIOUSNESS EXPRESS ITSELF?

"I believe consciousness is the way information feels when being processed."
– Mathematician Max Tegmark

When life came upon Earth, all creatures, even certain molecules evolved the ability to sense their environment.

As much as a gazelle will feel danger using her heightened senses of perception, water molecules can also sense their environment and retain "memories" as documented by the work of scientists Dr. Jacques Benveniste and Dr. Masaru Emoto.

Dr. Emoto studied water crystallization in relation to its emotional environment. In his laboratory, he subjected water samples, individually, to verbal affirmations. One sample received the verbal affirmation "I love you" while the other would be given "I hate you" statements. After several days, he compared the crystals of water of the two samples. The water crystals which had been exposed to the "I love you" affirmations were perfectly formed while the samples which had been put through a constant "I hate you" treatment showed an almost complete disorganization. He repeated this experiment many times in his career, with many different samples of water from around the world, always in a controlled environment, and each time the experiments yielded the same results. This showed that the crystallization was affected by the emotionally laden statements.

The work of Jacques Benveniste, a prominent researcher in immunology and hematology (his discovery of a platelet-activating factor in 1971 placed him on the list of candidates for the Nobel Prize in medicine), apparently demonstrated that water has memory. His experiments showed that water, which had been mixed with a substance, which then was completely extracted from the liquid, retained the properties associated with that substance. His discovery seemed to validate the principles of homeopathy medicine, which is based on treatments using extreme dilution of substances. Although his findings were published in the prestigious journal Nature, they are regarded as largely controversial albeit very intriguing.

If we look at our human condition and how we are built to thrive on Earth, we realize that we owe our ability to survive to our senses.
Our bodies equipped with very sophisticated sensors. Each of these sensors is linked to the commander in chief: The brain.

Each sense organ processes information from environmental stimuli, which in turn can be understood as a certain number of units of consciousness that are being interpreted by our brain, constantly, day and night.

Our commonly accepted senses are: sight, hearing, touch, smell, and taste. Each sense gives a dimensional coordinate about one piece of information from the material world which is also within the dimension of consciousness. The first five dimensional coordinates of a piece of information that are produced by our five senses help create the illusion of a three-dimensional world we live in. However, our first five senses do not give us any information on time. We can't hear time, nor can we see it, smell it or taste it, even less touch it, can we? When we look at a clock, we do not actually see time. We only see an interpretation of it.

So how do we get the information with regards to time? Well, we feel time. When we wait for something, we feel the time going by. How do we feel time, then? There is a sense we haven't spoken about yet: the 6th sense. The 6th sense (feeling) adds a dimension of time, because we "feel" it.

However, the 6th sense is not just limited to "feeling" time. The 6th sense does much more than that; in fact, our 6th sense is probably the best tool we have to understand our universe. The sixth sense is our ability to process on an unaware level all the information from the entire universe, which we have access to as we are a part of the universe. The 6th sense presents itself to our conscious mind as intuition.

I dare any scientist or doctor to deny they ever used their "6th sense" in their research or treatment choices. "The hunch" is something we all have experienced and used at one time or another in our life. In fact, I have met medical doctors and veterinarians who told me that their hunches are what have saved the patients they were treating, in emergency situations when time for rational thinking was not an option, as there was no time for logical deduction.

But I would like to go even further and propose that there are more than just six senses. We can detach ourselves from the analytical part of our brain and achieve "higher states" of awareness. Meditation is a common technique to do so. For others, it is prayer or even singing. What it does is that it gives permission to the ego to take a step back, allowing a prejudice and judgement free openness to emerge. When this occurs, we can input information from sources beyond what can be processed by the first six senses. This does not occur naturally, as does the sensory input from the five senses but must be learned.

What does that mean? It means that we learn, step by step, to discover other senses and come to realize that these senses allow us to access a greater part of consciousness, the mind of all in an information-theoretic way. We saw in chapter 4, that Wheeler conceives the universe as being information-theoretic. If consciousness encompasses all information, consciousness becomes the "mind of all", the mind of the universe.

Postulate for example a 7th sense, which we will call "knowing". This sense grounds us into the universe, by a "knowing" that we are part of it. Some could liken this to faith. This is not a religious faith, but more like a natural faith, which makes us, understand the order of things.

Then let's envision the 8th sense that we will call "connectedness". It gives us a sense of belonging to something greater than just ourselves while being that greater thing at the same time. This is a common element of profound meditative state and the near-death experience.

Finally, the 9th sense or 9th dimensional coordinate would be total awareness, encompassing all the other senses at once and giving us access to consciousness in its whole.

Total awareness implies that we have access to all these dimensional coordinates that constitute ultimate reality, which is consciousness as a whole.

Have you ever wondered why our universe has so many limitations? For example, the speed of light as a speed limit travelling within the universe, the absolute zero, the Singularity, and the mind-blowing infinity concept? They are all based upon human observations and calculations using only our first five dimensional senses, which create the illusion of the 3D world we live in.

Buddha said, "The mind who perceives the limitation IS the limitation".

Some scientists are trying to explain our universe through mathematical calculations, which suggest that a 4D star might have imploded into a singular moment, thus creating our "Big Bang," sputtering out our 3D universe in the form of a hologram. Many others are stating that the original void was actually filled with energy in the form of the

Higgs field that eventually gave birth to quantum fluctuations, which made possible the incredible inflation that we went through leading to the continuing expansion of our universe. As we attempt to access the many models of the universe, we can either assume that one idea is the correct one or postulate that all models are correct.

Why? Because our consciousness is limited by our observable senses, which results in "observable" and mathematical semi-solutions, ultimately leading to more questions. That is in fact the current situation in theoretical physics. There are solutions which work extremely well in the abstract world of mathematics but they still don't answer the main questions. These unanswered questions include the lack of a unified theory of the subatomic world and observable reality as well as the fundamental structure of the universe before and after the Big Bang.

Why again? Because we have been using our first five senses and our left-brain, our logical and Cartesian brain, to create these models. We still haven't really tried to expand our perceptions to a much broader field of consciousness. Ancient philosophies such as the Tao have come to pretty much the same conclusion as modern mathematics and physics just by using their sense of "knowing".

For example, the Tao Te Ching, a five-thousand-word Chinese text written in the 6th century BC, attributed to Lao-Tzu, teaches us that everything derives from the nameless void, but that this nameless void is not empty. It is a full vacuum.

The Tao represents the natural way we process and understand the universe. It is the universe made conscious through us, because we live it through all our senses. Yet, our five senses constrict us into a partial view of the whole. (It sounds very much like the collapsing of the quantum wave function.)

Why is it so difficult to fathom that it's not a question of *"before there was nothing, then there was everything"* but rather a question of *"everything has always been here"* and consciousness could very well be one of the major components, if not the whole of that everything. Whether time and space are all spread out and there is no singularity or even no big bang, or time and space were created right at the start of the big bang, consciousness has already been a key element of the universe, appearing at the first quantum fluctuation and containing everything else. Imagine a Russian doll. The smallest doll inside is our 3D reality, the doll containing our 3D reality is the 4D space-time continuum, the dolls after that may even contain more dimensions as discovered in the Super String Theory manifolds, and last but not least, comes the biggest doll of all: consciousness, containing everything else.

In this regard, the quantum gravity model of Wheeler-deWitt, the no boundary model of Hawkins and Hartle and the Wheeler Participatory universe model are all correct, as the multi-dimensional universe which exists beyond our understandings using our ordinary senses might be a fusion of all these interpretations (and more).

Physicist David Deutsch said in one of his Ted Talks that a theory becomes solid if calculations always yield the same results and interpretations do not vary. If a theory has too many variations in explanations, yet still yields the same results, chances are the theory is not valid.

With all these explanations and interpretations of our universe's beginning given by quantum mechanics and cosmology, we have tremendous amount of variations. This suggest they are all wrong and the universe has no beginning, giving credence to the causal loop theories.

Before we accept these causal loop theories which negate the concept of a "beginning", I think we must first reconsider our notion of time. We must further develop our understanding of how time is interpreted through our brain. Using my seventh sense, I "feel" that it is where the solution lies.

As a medium, I use the part of my brain which allows me to filter consciousness in a much richer way. As a result, I have considerable experimental evidence obtained by my seventh sense which supports my "feeling" that our notion of time is so distorted that it is almost impossible for us to clearly interpret the mathematics behind it all.

Why do our brains want to find a beginning and an end to everything? Because we are stuck in a time constricted, 4D universe.

Greek philosopher Plato offers his allegory of The Cave: prisoners are kept chained in a cave, always facing the same wall. A fire behind them casts shadows on the wall they face. Prisoners think what they see is reality. They do not question it. But one day, one prisoner is freed and turns around. He is told that what he is seeing now IS reality. But the fire's intense light burns his eyes, and he does not want to believe that this could be reality. He is dragged by force outside The Cave and after acclimating to the sun's light, discovers a whole, entirely new reality filled with beauty. Naturally, he runs back to The Cave to tell his fellow prisoners. But the sun's light temporarily blinds him and when his friends see that he has been blinded by the light they don't believe what he says about this entirely different reality that is so beautiful. They decide he presents a real danger to their peace and should be eliminated.

What Plato demonstrates with his allegory is that, not only are there other realities for us to discover, but most importantly, that our brain is the limitation, because our interpretation of our universe is based on what we observe with our first five senses.

In one witness account after another, for decades, tens of thousands of people who have had an NDE (near-death experience, as defined in our prologue) and have come back to life have said that there are many other realities much more vibrant than ours. Unfortunately, like in the allegory of The Cave, they haven't been taken seriously and much too often their stories have been rejected by the medical teams that brought them back to life, and by society. It is commonly thought that they must have hallucinated their experiences because of the lack of oxygen in their brain, they say, or because of the drugs and medicine they have been given. The scientific community doesn't want to believe these eyewitness accounts of other realities because they represent a danger for the established truth. Thankfully today, we are starting to open our eyes and our mind to the scientific paradigm shift that allows these amazing stories to be accounted for and ultimately studied.

That very mind that is writing what I am writing now knows that if I accept to expand and try to reach the 6th, 7th, 8th and 9th dimensional coordinates, I might be able to grasp the idea of *Everythingness*. Though it is extraordinary to be able to compute mathematically all that we see and to hold mathematics as a true language, never will mathematical language be able to find the answer to the "who", "where" and "why" questions. Why are we here? Where are we going when we die? Who is at the origin of all this?

Why are we so limited? Why are there so many diverse models and answers to these questions? Because the very consciousness that creates it all is trying to explain its own existence through a limited processor: the left-brain of the mind-brain unit.

Chapter 9
SUBCONSCIOUS BRAIN vs CONSCIOUS BRAIN

"The conscious mind is not at the center of the action in the brain; instead, it is far out on a distant edge, hearing but whispers of the activity."
— David Eagleman, neuroscientist, adjunct associate professor at Stanford University in the department of Psychiatry & Behavioral Sciences, in "Incognito: The Secret Lives of the Brain"

At the beginning of this book, I very schematically and simplistically described our brain as a "left-brain" mind unit and a "right-brain" mind unit. It is of course far more complicated than that; as a matter of fact, it is as complicated as the billions of neural connections in this Jell-O like gray matter blob.

Dr. David Eagleman describes the brain functions linked to our daily actions as more subconscious than conscious. He demonstrates that most of the things we do every day are in fact deeply embedded in our subconscious mind. He even goes further stating that we do not really have free will in our actions.

According to his theory, our neurons have created millions of pathways for each action, using DNA information, but also experience. When we make a conscious decision, we are in fact totally influenced by the way our subconscious perceives our environment and by our body chemistry at the moment we make this decision. To him our conscious mind has in fact a much smaller role than predicted. Our conscious mind thinks it is in control, but it is not.

The interesting part is that in this scenario, consciousness and sub-consciousness are equally placed "inside" the brain, and occur only because the brain actively processes information in the form of electrical impulses and chemical reactions. According to Dr. Eagleman, the minimal role consciousness (as defined as awareness) has in our daily life is what places it far from the action. Once again, in this model, it is the actual action of processing information that results in thoughts becoming consciousness (or sub-consciousness).

This model clearly outlines that our brain, as complicated and sophisticated as it is, as being very limited in its global assessment of its surroundings, let alone the universe. Why? Because it is processing information based on DNA and sensory perceptions limited to our first five senses.

David Eagleman tells the interesting story of a woman who was in a terrible motorcycle accident and lost the "emotional part" of her brain. Her rational brain was intact and she could process information in a very logical and methodological way. Yet, faced with a choice, she was unable to feel what would be the better of two given situations, based on all the information on hand.

Take away the emotions and we become incapable of functioning even in the most simplistic yet important situations of our daily life. "What will I buy to cook dinner tonight?" becomes an impossible task to accomplish if we lose our emotional "feeling" part of our brain.

In our daily life, our brain lives by the quantum principle of uncertainty described in chapter 5. With all the sensory inputs our brain receives at every moment, once it chooses to focus on one part of the information gathered, the other parts become impossible to process precisely, always giving a restricted image of reality, and sometimes impeding actions. *"Once you begin deliberating about where your fingers are jumping on the piano keyboard, you can no longer pull off the piece."* - David Eagleman "Incognito - The secret lives of the brain

When we understand that the brain has as many as nine senses, and that we are all connected to the universe by a universal consciousness, then suddenly we understand that it is not emotions vs rational mind, it's not subconscious vs conscious mind, it's not alive vs dead, and it's not inside the brain vs outside the brain. These dualities reflect an underlying unity of the existence of everything and the superposition of states of everything. It's about this uncertainty, where one can't really go without the other. In order to function in this reality, we must focus on one aspect of it at a time, otherwise, we can't comprehend it and master it. The truth is that the universe is comprised of a unitary sea of information. When we only use the five senses of our brain, we create these dualities (among others) in our effort to understand reality. However, the unity of the universe is, in fact our reality, similar to the Yin and the Yang, creating a whole.

In chapter 11, we will see that a brain deprived of its rational thinking capabilities allows more in-depth exploration of consciousness, than a brain deprived of its emotional feelings like we just saw. The duality of the treatment of the information only applies to the physical and matter condition of our being.

Chapter 10
CONSCIOUSNESS FIRST OR HUMAN BRAIN FIRST?

"The nature of an egg is determined by what it contains and not what lays it"
– Alun, owner and blogger of Greesleeves Hub

The nature of consciousness and its relation to our brain likely is the oldest human quest in the world: What came first, consciousness or the brain?

Let's review the three following hypotheses, and see if we can make up our mind:

Hypothesis 1
Awareness that allows the processing of consciousness comes about when brain cells, neurons, start interacting with one another in utero between the 24th and 28th weeks of gestation, and ceases to exist when we die and there is no more brain activity. This is the most commonly accepted explanation in today's world of medicine and science.

Hypothesis 2
Awareness that allows the processing of consciousness comes about when brain cells, neurons, start interacting with one another in utero between the 24th and 28th weeks of gestation, but does not cease to exist when we die. It just changes its state of existence. This is a long debated theory that we can find in many spiritual and religious beliefs.

Hypothesis 3

Consciousness exists before the emergence of awareness in the developing embryo. It gets processed by a new brain forming in the fetus and experiences all kinds of interpretations. It acquires at the same time more information, which is filtered by this new brain whose genetic code and experience create a unique reality. It continues to be processed by that same brain until the person dies, at which point consciousness, as a whole, continues to exist while retaining the data and information from the life it has experienced with this human body (or animal body, or thermostat, or… you get the picture.)

Now let's go back to our question: "What came first, consciousness or the brain, the egg or the chicken?"

While you could arguably say that this is a futile question, there is a reason that I pose it. Stay with me, your open-mindedness is about to pay off, I assure you. The comparison in this particular case denotes similar concepts and raises a very profound question of evolution.

"The nature of an egg is determined by what it contains and not by what lays it." In this sentence, we can easily understand the parallel one could make between consciousness and the egg. The nature of consciousness is determined by what it contains (data, emotional knowledge, dimensional information, lots of zeros and ones etc.). The nature of consciousness is not determined by what processes it (like a brain for example).

In the hypothetical case we could place a cuckoo's egg in a surrogate magpie body, *(or even simply in the magpie's nest, as it is exactly what happens in nature)*, we would observe that when the egg is laid, it is still a cuckoo's egg. It has not changed.

As the magpie will adopt the egg and will make it hers and the chick will identify itself as a magpie, the egg will remain a cuckoo's egg and the chick, a cuckoo's chick. The information is preserved.

Similarly, let's trace consciousness through the brain: the information, processed by the brain, will go through unaltered. A photon of light that left the sun about seven minutes ago, hits the retina of a being that is alive and a being that is dead. In one case the photon is analyzed by the brain of the living being and is translated by electrical impulses into light and seeing. In the other case, there is no "translation" as the being is dead, but the photon still has hit the eye of the being, no matter his state of existence. The information of the photon remains true. I postulate that this is not only true for a photon, but it is actually valid for everything, including the information-theoretic personality and memory of any being.

How do we declare death in traditional medical terms? Death is "a permanent cessation of all vital functions" according to Merriam-Webster dictionary. In reality, there are three types of deaths: clinical death, legal death and information-theoretic death. Clinical death is defined by the cessation of all vital functions of a person. Legal death is when someone is declared clinically dead or someone has been missing for years and is declared dead on a document.

And then, there is information-theoretic death. What can this be? Information-theoretic death is the obliteration, the total destruction of what makes a person, her personality, her memory with no possibility of getting it back (supposedly). Say that a person dies from a heart attack. The person is declared clinically dead and eventually legally dead. Yet, it takes a while before the brain cells start to deteriorate to a point of no return. During this time, the person can be clinically and legally dead, but is not information-theoretically dead.

Some people have recourse to cryopreservation techniques to conserve their body after death. They are clinically dead. Yet, thanks to the cryonic processes that prevent their brain cells from deteriorating after death, the information-theoretic part of their being is, in theory, still preserved. When a person has had a near-death experience, they were clinically dead but not information-theoretically dead, which explains how they can return to life with their personality and memories intact.

So, the idea behind this is that what makes a person truly alive, is directly information-theoretic derived. It's exactly what I've been striving to demonstrate all along in this book, but I am going even further by saying that the total obliteration of the self after death is utterly impossible.

The scientific evidence clearly suggests that the information-theoretic essence of any being is encoded forever in the memory of our universal consciousness. The second we start processing consciousness through our senses and our brain, we contribute to the information-theoretic existence of ourselves within the universe and become one with everything. The body can be discarded at the moment of clinical and legal death, but the information-theoretic death is, in my opinion, impossible. If my understanding of the scientific evidence coupled with my own mediumship experiments is correct, then consciousness is the information theoretic of everything and is stored in the "cloud". Brains (among other things) download from and upload to, this universe based equivalent of the cloud on a constant basis. Once the brain is dead, its local storage and processing systems are destroyed, but all the information the brain has processed in and out is preserved in the "cloud" with the rest of the universe's data. And that is where we can find our lost loved ones, to talk to them! Literally "in the cloud".

Our brain interprets consciousness with its own frames of reference. It gives a rendition of consciousness and its contents based on its own configuration and its own genetic codes; all brought about by bodily sensory perceptions. Yet, all information remains unaltered, while new information created by the processing of consciousness through our brain is returned to the whole. As much as the information of a photon that hits our retina is true to the information of that same photon born some 13.8 billion years ago, the information-theoretic essence of a dead person is true to the information-theoretic essence of that same person when he/she was alive.

So how do we know what's the true nature of information? How can we directly perceive consciousness unaltered by our brain?

There seems to be no way to objectively qualify and quantify consciousness. Super quantum computers are trying to achieve this. We certainly discussed the idea of units of consciousness in this book, but we have yet to provide a reliable scale of units like meters for distance and seconds for time.

I think this is simply because we do not have the language to express it yet. Models such as Michio Kaku's are a great start and a definite hope we are working in the right direction.

The problem is that even the practice of interpretation of information itself creates new data which is released into the dimension of consciousness and contributes to its expansion. A never-ending process.

If we presuppose that there are many humanlike civilizations in the universe and that they all filter and interpret consciousness more or less the same way we do, this could very well corroborate the idea of a participatory universe. Would a few 1.5 sextillion hypothetically habitable planets in the universe (that's 15 with 20 zeros behind) be enough to create so much data feeding and indefinitely processing consciousness that consciousness would actually create everything?

We can find this particular idea in the Gaia theory, also called Biogeochemical Hypothesis.

The Gaia theory argues that everything and everyone on Earth is interconnected to the point that Earth is a single living organism that can self-regulate to sustain life. It supports the notion of a participatory universe.

Take the cloud formations over oceans for example, unpredictable by nature, because they follow deterministic chaos dynamics*; yet, cloud formations over oceans are not just random physical and chemical phenomena, they are in fact, mainly the result of an organic process by oceanic algae. Algae release sulfur as a waste gas in the air, which in turn triggers condensation of water, creating enough rainwater to feed our rivers and sustain life. These are the environmental conditions which lead to cloud formations which in turn creates rainwater which supports life, all according to mathematical principles, all one interconnected system. The specific organism Algae can be seen as processing and releasing data which is its particular part of the complex system. *The chaos theory is a mathematical theory that shows that predictable systems cannot stay foreseeable more than a certain period of time after which they will act totally randomly. Chaos theory is used in meteorology and in traffic control to name just a couple of applications.

The idea of processing data and releasing it constantly, thus contributing to its self-expansion, is just a tiny extrapolation of the Gaia theory.

There are problems however, with the theory that consciousness is expressed through sentient beings. In this case, consciousness would absolutely need humanlike or animal-like life forms in the universe to create itself and perpetuate itself. At the same time, this might actually explain the cause of all genetic mutations in the history of the evolution of all creatures on Earth and elsewhere; thus, consciousness could be also the cause for all creations of all time. Consciousness as the underlying creative force in biological systems would mean that genetic errors and mutations are part of that same creative force, leading to unexpected new creations through the processes of genetic mutation.

On the other hand, if consciousness is at the origin of our universe, and does not depend on thinking beings to come to existence but simply benefits from their contribution in information, this solves the problem. Consciousness could then exist prior to or at the creation of the universe or just as its first quantum fluctuation appeared, which of course is a time when no living beings existed. At the same time, it consolidates the intrinsic role of consciousness as a dimension of our universe. Thinking beings, in this theory, contribute to consciousness's content, and consequently have a small but not negligible role in its expansion. This is unlike the role thinking beings play in creating time and space. The difference in the two theories is simply over the relationship between the universal consciousness and its expression in material reality.

In both theories, the fact that processing consciousness helps refine the building blocks of our very nature is evidence that consciousness is much more than awareness created by brain activity. In both theories, it does exist inherently but also acquires information from all sentient beings.

There exists an anecdotal saying that gives the same compelling conclusion about the inherent nature of consciousness. "If a tree falls in the forest, and if no one is present to hear the tree fall, will it make a sound?"

What is a sound? A sound is a vibration that propagates in the air (or another medium) and can be heard by one's ears. The vibration, the wave that travels through the ambient nature, hits our eardrums with sound energy, kinetic energy from the air, energy created by the sound wave. That sound energy is then turned into electromagnetic signals traveling through our brain axons to our neurons in charge of interpreting them as sound.

So, if no one is in the forest, there will be no interpretation of the vibration of the air created by the tree falling. However, the vibration will exist no matter what and will propagate in the air. The existence of that vibration, to begin with, is what would enable a potential eardrum to capture it and a brain to interpret it as a sound. If there is no sound wave, there is no sound interpretation. The absence of a brain constitutes no obstacle for the existence of the sound wave. The vibration exists but is simply unobserved.

Now, replace the word vibration by consciousness (remember consciousness is information), and eardrum by all our senses. You will see that the comparison yields the same result. If there is no brain to process consciousness (information), there is no interpretation of it, but it does not deny the existence of consciousness (information).

Armed with these two anecdotal yet profound comparisons, to which hypothesis do you think consciousness relates the best?

Does consciousness arise from the emergence of awareness in a 24-week-old fetus and vanish at the point of death? Does consciousness come about in utero but keep going after death, simply changing its state? Or, does it become obvious that consciousness has always been present and will always be as it is a fundamental building block of the universe? The third hypothesis seems the most plausible to me. For all the grieving parents, sons, daughters, families and friends, it is important to understand that consciousness, scientifically speaking, must be self-contained and autonomous in the universe. All that our loved ones once were, still is, as they remain mapped in the dimension of consciousness. Their information-theoretic essence is forever present. Not only is it still mapped, but it could also be accessible and retrievable by a third person. This could take the form of a spiritual vision experienced by a loved one, or could be facilitated by a medium. Perhaps technical devices such as *EVP technology could play a role in retrieving the information that is the essence of a "departed" loved one. Of course, they are only departed from our perspective, they exist forever in the informational reality that is part of the universal consciousness. *(*EVP: Electronic Voice Phenomena, which are recorded recognizable voices that appear in the context of background of white noises.)*

We also envisioned that the way our lost loved ones interpreted consciousness gives birth to new information that becomes part of the self-contained data, as well. This is the reason why anyone (trained, or not in the technique of remote viewing or Spiritual Sight), can retrieve information from "nowhere". In reality, information is not coming from nowhere but from everywhere.

Chapter 11
PROPERTIES OF CONSCIOUSNESS

"[...] And I remember thinking, there is no way I would be able to squeeze the enormousness of myself back inside this tiny little body [...]"
– Dr. Jill Bolte Taylor, neuroanatomist, while experiencing a stroke on her left-brain.

The idea I am offering is that consciousness is a wonderful thing that we can experience through our body and its sensors and processors.

Billions of bits of information bombard us at any given time. Only a few thousands are filtered by our left-brain, as we discussed in chapter 2, whereas our right-brain does a much better job of feeling how incredibly vast, diverse and constantly expanding consciousness is.

Consciousness permeates everything. It is the ultimate Akashic Record, a universal and cosmic memory that is encoded in the very fabric of the universe. Coming from the Vedic Hinduism (the oldest Hinduist philosophy) and the Vedantic Hinduism (the classic form of Hinduism), and from the sacred Sanskrit language, the word Akasha successively means "open space" or "emptiness", then "sky" or "space". I can't help myself but to establish a link between Akasha and Tao, which both originally built upon the notion of "full vacuum". This is the notion that everything is born from nothing and that the vacuum contains everything. All the necessary energy is present in the primordial vacuum of the universe. All the information of the universe that is ready to expand is contained into and contains this full vacuum. Our teleological paradox shows up again as we struggle to understand how a vacuum can contain everything and yet be contained in that same vacuum

    The idea of Akasha was then occidentalized around the 19th century to give birth to the term Akashic Record. It represents the idea that all the information, emotions, events, and all data are thought to be encoded in an astral plane. This is not far from the idea that consciousness is a dimension like time and space with retrievable data.

    Consciousness is so vast. It contains everything. For someone who would have lost the ability to use her rational left-brain, or someone who is going through a near-death experience (NDE), it would feel impossible to fit all this knowledge, all this space-time-information, the very essence of the universe in such a tiny body. In these type of situations, consciousness seems to be the observer and the observed at the same time. The idea of a consciousness creator and recipient of all states of things agrees with the quantum principle of superposition: As soon as we try to funnel down the information it becomes impossible to apprehend it in its entirety.

    So many parallels can be established between scientific principles and experiences such as Dr. Bolte Taylor's. However, we do not have to rely on these spontaneous experiences which cannot be replicated by their very accidental nature. People who are trained in meditation, remote viewing or in the techniques of extrasensory perception have also made the same observations.

So, consciousness seems to have quantum properties; but is that its only similarity with physical phenomena? Expansion also seems to be a common denominator between the universe and consciousness. Dr. Bolte Taylor describes her stroke experience as feeling her body having no limits. She recalls not being able to see the boundaries of her body. One of the theories of the existence of the universe, described in chapter 4, describes the cosmos as a "no boundary universe". I find the similarity uncanny.

Many human experiences, as we have seen, find their parallel in the descriptions of our universe's modus operandi and in its laws. Of course, not one of these experiences individually proves anything, but the fact that they occur throughout human societies and are related to the matter of consciousness must give consciousness a preponderant place in the future of science exploration.

Consciousness is our final frontier. It expands and yet is self-contained and seems autonomous. Bits of it can be filtered by many beings at the same time. And if bits of it can be filtered, then there must be a unit of consciousness. We cannot observe time. We can only see the effects of time, or the interpretation of time; yet we have found a way to quantify time to make it work in our equations. In the same vein, there must be a way to quantify consciousness.

Let's review what we have learned about consciousness:

- consciousness is information, data.
- consciousness manifests through beings and instruments with different degrees of awareness.
- consciousness allows interpretations of itself.
- consciousness contains space and time and expands as new information and data is created at any given time.
- consciousness is "it from bit" and could hopefully be quantified and perhaps quantized.
- consciousness allows us to experience love and loss and a complete array of emotions, which are in return self-contained as information and data in the dimension of consciousness.
- If no beings existed in the universe, consciousness would still exist by being part of it or by being its whole; but its degree of expansion might be calculated at a different pace.
- Quantum computers attempt to replicate consciousness. These computers are built on conceptualizations that originate from human interpretation. Their computing capacities are phenomenal, but as yet, they cannot recreate consciousness. They can only contribute to its expansion by simulating its essence.
- If consciousness is inherent to the universe, then bodily death on Earth means only the end of interpretation of consciousness by this particular body and brain; yet, the information-theoretic essence pertaining to this specific body and brain

and all the information filtered during the life of this particular body, remain in the dimension of consciousness. It is therefore potentially accessible to experiencers and instruments.

We have to face the scientific facts: consciousness is really much more than awareness due to brain activity. So, armed with this evidence, we are now ready to tackle the big questions!

1) Can we continue experiencing consciousness when we die? From our own point of view and the point of view of those who stay?

2) Is consciousness truly a retrievable form of data by other living beings and by technical instruments?

3) How is consciousness processed by cognitively impaired people, or intellectually disabled people, and by those who are in a coma?

4) Are we processing consciousness when we are supposedly "unconscious" in medical terms or simply asleep?

5) Can consciousness interact with us the way we interact with it? In other words, can consciousness manifest spontaneously without our freewill and the intentional processing of our neuronal circuitry or that of an instrument? As in spontaneous after death communication – ADC, or during NDEs.

6) Is consciousness responsible for all the good deeds and all the terrible events happening on Earth and in the universe?

7) Does consciousness create and destroy or does it bear all possibilities at once and we humans choose to apply one or the other?

These are the questions that we will attempt to answer in the next chapters.

Chapter 12
TO BE OR NOT TO BE
Can we continue experiencing consciousness after death?

"[...] Sure, he that made us with such large discourse,
Looking before and after, gave us not
That capability and God-like reason
To fust in us unused. [...]"
— Shakespeare in Hamlet-Act 4, Scene 4

The opening phrase of the soliloquy of the Nunnery scene in Hamlet's "To be or not to be, that is the question" is probably one of the most famous phrases of the English literature.

In the play, Prince Hamlet is torn between two possibilities: face his turmoil and act with vengeance or end his pain and suffering by committing suicide.

He is particularly consumed by the idea that his soul could still face some kind of torment after his suicide, because, to him, not using the power of his brain to reason is the trait of a "beast" and not a human.

This leads us to the 1st question mentioned in the previous chapter: "Can we continue experiencing consciousness when we die?" From our own point of view and from the point of view of those who stay?"

After all, "Sure, he that made us with such large discourse,
Looking before and after, gave us not
That capability and God-like reason
To fust in us unused."

Yes, after all, our brain has the capability to process and reason, and it would be a shame not to use it, wouldn't it? Yet, if our brain did not exist anymore, if we died, would we still exist? If there were no brain to process the "data" would the data still exist, in "the cloud"?

If there were absolutely no brain, anywhere in the universe, to process the latent information, would it mean that no information would exist? "I think, therefore I am," let's not forget what Descartes said!

The answer is simple. I think we are so very lucky that we can exist without prejudice in both cases! Prince Hamlet need not have worried!

Being alive and being dead are only two superposed states of the same system. And the system is called: Life! (Remember the Schrodinger's cat experiment in our chapter 5?)

In the many accounts of NDEs (near-death experiences), people describe experiences of "leaving their bodies;" yet they are still aware of who they are and of their identity. They describe feeling an "immense love too big and too strong to be contained in one's body." They chronicle a sensation of "expansion", of "being part of something greater"

and "merging with the light;" a light extremely intense, yet not blinding.
They also recount perceiving time as non-existent, not even being a factor in what they experience.

Does that sound any bit familiar to you? Let's see what we have learned from our previous chapters about the origin of the universe and the postulate of consciousness pre-existing it, and let's compare:

- Very aware of everything = consciousness as a whole
- Love too big to be contained = hidden variables and inflation
- Expanding = post Big Bang
- Being part of something greater = being part of the expansion
- Merging with the light = particles merging to create matter, releasing energy (we are literally stardust)
- Time non-existent = time all spread out (outside view of the universe)
- Leaving their body and being anywhere at will = the concepts of quantum superposition.

These are very convincing parallels strongly suggesting that during the near-death experience, for example, persons directly experience the fundamental laws of physics as they apply to the universe. This makes sense because we humans, or any being in the universe for that matter, are built following the model of the universe itself. Not only are we part of it, but we are it!

Furthermore, if we can have an outside view of our universe through consciousness, that means that consciousness contains time and space and indeed appeared first. In science and particularly in quantum physics, an outside view or a bird's eye view is what defines the wholeness of reality. Each one of us experiences a 1st person view of reality which represents as we saw in chapter 5 on quantum mechanics, one outcome of the many possible outcomes of realities. Yet the true reality encompasses all the outcomes of everything and only an outside view of the universe would allow the viewer to "see" them all at once. Thus, if consciousness contains all time and all space, it can act like an outside viewer and perceive all possible outcomes of everything.

Every day, our brain computes millions of bits of information. Some actions require critical thinking but most are done automatically. The information exchanges that go from all our sensors to the brain and back are computed involuntarily; we do not need to be aware of these mechanisms. However, when we learn to ride a bike for the first time, for example, our brain creates new neuronal pathways in order for us to actually master the bike ride. We become good riders by repeatedly pedaling, keeping our balance, feeling how much we need to move the handle bar right or left to slightly adapt to the direction of the road and the terrain. The same happens when driving a car. It requires critical thinking at first.

However, the beauty of the brain ensures that once we have created these paths, we no longer require critical thinking to perform known actions. How many of us have driven home from work, subsequently having no recollection of how we got there and how long it took? This is because our brain was on "auto-pilot". Our brain was in an altered state of consciousness. We were in "the zone." When you are in "the zone" or in a meditative state, you need not critical thinking to perform actions; you can actually drift into a completely different scene, or world and still perform the action on hand, because the information is processed automatically. Because the truthfulness property of the information is always preserved, the critical thinking part of the brain needed to perform a repetitive action or an action known to our circuitry becomes useless, leaving more space and freedom for sensory exploration.

In medical terms, we could say that you are performing an action unconsciously. However, I prefer to use the term unaware. When we are in the "zone" or in a meditative state, we are still very much evolving through the dimension of consciousness, albeit unaware of, and inattentive to our physical reality. This allows us to expand into space, time and consciousness. This is what we commonly call an "altered state" of consciousness. It is altered because it is heightened. Being in the "zone" is only another word for meditating. Meditation is a word that can scare people, but it is only a way to calm the left part of our mind-brain unit that we talked about in our chapter 1. Once the left part of our brain is almost practically silent, our right-brain can freely process information without being analyzed by our left-brain. In doing so, we then expand ourselves in many ways and directions like an NDE experiencer would do. Time and space are no longer constraints. We fill space and time with our awareness and expand into the dimension of consciousness.

If we had a deadly accident on the road going from work to home, we would expand completely into space, time and consciousness, retaining all information spread out and acquired; subsequently supplying consciousness with more personal data, readily available to any sensor in the universe. This would explain why many people experience ADC (Spontaneous After Death Communication) from loved ones. The information is readily available at any given time to any consciousness sensor in the universe. The human brain is such a consciousness sensor.

So, whether we are alive or not, we evolve in a constantly expanding dimension that contains "us" in an informational theoretic manner. Whether Prince Hamlet decides to stay and face his angst or makes the irrevocable decision to end his life, he still will experience all the consequences of his actions within the expanding realm of conscious information.

Chapter 13
IS CONSCIOUSNESS TRULY RETRIEVABLE DATA?
Can we interact with consciousness?

"History shows us that it is a bad idea to consistently say that we have now reached the end of the Solar System and there is nothing beyond what we already know"
– Konstantin Batygin – Caltech Assistant Professor of Planetary Science about his discovery of a ninth planet in our solar system.

In this chapter, we are going to talk about how information can be retrieved by our human brains, remotely and in "non-controlled" environments. The term "controlled" refers to the scientific method of experimenting by which possibilities of interferences and/or pollution from an outside source of the experiment are minimized.

Remote viewing experiments done in a non-controlled environment are not the experimental proof that upon which science often depends. However, the essence of science is the direct observation of phenomena, so the documentation of observations according to a rigorous protocol is in fact the essence of the scientific method. Furthermore, the sheer amount of evidence they generate and the striking results they show are such that they are impossible to ignore or dismiss. Still, science has yet to find a rational explanation for them and has yet to replicate them in a controlled environment. This work has been done at PEAR, the

Princeton University Department of Engineering's Anomalous Research lab, but more work needs to be done.

I will explain why I think some of these experiences are impossible to replicate in a controlled or even in a non-controlled experiment. It is because of their indeterministic nature. As in all quantum phenomena, you can observe them happening in real time but if you try to focus on a particular point of the experiment, you will lose the ability to grasp it in its entirety.

Let's revisit for a moment the accounts of NDErs. We can notice a common thread that weaves through the extensive collection of NDE stories. This common core experience does not depend upon sex, age, race, geo-location, health, social upbringing, or belief system. This common thread that I will call the STEM* contains the ideas of detachment and expansion. (*Not to be confused with the S.T.E.M. – science, technology, engineering and mathematics that we find in our education system. Interestingly enough though, that S.T.E.M. is directly linked to our left-brain capabilities, whereas the STEM that I am about to discuss emanates from our right-brain and possibly from the core essence of consciousness.)

Every single NDE account refers to a feeling of being detached from the body, regardless of what happens next and what is felt or seen during the NDE itself. Sometimes this detachment presents as an out of body experience, other times it manifests as a transcendent union with the universe.

As previously described in chapter 12, NDE accounts also describe a sensation of filling the entire space and time, so much so that time and space themselves become irrelevant.

That feeling of detachment is very important because it denotes a sensation that cannot be felt in a normal state of awareness. This perception of the 1st person being centered in one's body and one's head is what creates the illusion of being "us".

Those who are trained in deep meditation can also feel this strong and life altering sensation of being separated from the body (OBE – out-of-body experience) or mystical union with the universe. This frequently results in personal transformation.

Of course, we have no way of measuring the level of detachment on a scale, but according to the millions of accounts of NDE reported in a 1992 Gallup poll, the separation is powerful, and almost complete. However, an NDEr typically finds a reason and a way to "go back" to his or her body. NDEs are so common in this era of advanced cardiac resuscitation that according to Jeffrey Long MD, cofounder of ndef.org, there occur an average of 774 NDEs each day, just in the USA, which is not counting any other part of the world.

This reminds me of a fascinating book I read when I was in my early 20s: "Les Thanatonautes" by Bernard Weber (in English, The Thanatonauts – from the Greek Thanatos – Divinities of Death). In this book a team of young and bold scientists embarks on a journey to the outer-most reach of consciousness, to the tenuous frontier between life and death using their medical skills and armed with the Tibetan Book of the Dead, The Egyptian Book of the Dead, and with other mythologies as well as sacred and religious texts.

What they discover is a world with several layers and levels. Each time they "go" they can only rely on that silver cord that links their "soul" to their body. But it is only so stretchable. The reader wonders if they will they cave in under the pressure and the desire to attain the last level, knowing that their silver cord might snap, and they would never come back? This particular analogy in the book seems to depict very well the sensation NDErs feel when they have to find the way to come back, sometimes it seems, against their own wishes to stay.

A famous blockbuster movie called "Flatliners" shows the tribulations of death travelers in a rather dark light. As they are purposely "killed" by their medical student friends, to discover the afterlife, most of them find themselves in situations where they have to make things right from a past memory. For one of them, the "trips" actually become very dangerous. Yet as difficult and even perilous as their endeavor becomes, they keep pushing forward. It gets harder and harder to be brought back to life, as they can't resist the impulse to extend the number of minutes and seconds their heart is stopped before their friends can shock it to bring them back.

Unlike in the movie "Flatliners", the Thanatonauts' return to life is not contingent upon the help of a colleague armed with a defibrillator, but more on their capacity to resist the urge to let go as their conscious being expands in a feeling of total bliss outside their body.

These fictional examples serve to illustrate how NDErs, while being "detached", continue to be aware of their surroundings. They are able to record every detail of their earthly experience from a reference point in a time that seems to be completely different than our time frame.

There also seems to be a notion of not caring for one's own body, and "looking at it" with no worry or fear of being away from it. The body seems useless and ultimately even a burden.

This detachment and the expansion, the STEM of the near-death experience is also the STEM described in psychic work and Controlled Remote Viewing work to a certain degree.

Psychic readers and controlled remote viewers use detachment techniques to bypass their busy left-brain in order to access information in a different way. The information becomes untainted by the reader's or the viewer's interpretive "baggage" that is ego based and consists of acquired knowledge and DNA layers of preconceived ideas. By using detachment techniques, the reader or the viewer lets through the true information from the universal consciousness.

Every single piece of information that comes after the detachment process is one leaf on the tree of life. Billions (an almost infinite number really) of leaves are attached to the same stem. Each leaf represents one real-life experience taking place, one possibility from among a multitude of others (quantum physics). From afar all leaves look the same, but on a closer look, each leaf is unique. Yet all the leaves together are creating a beautiful tree of life.

In Buddhism, the original Pali Canon is a collection of scriptures that include rules for monks, discourses from Buddha and metaphysical and philosophical texts, which are all written on thin slices of wood and palm leaves, that are superposed one on top of another. To be able to find one specific type of information one would have to first know where to look in the categories (STEM) to make his or her way to the specific leaf where the requested text is written. This interesting system of data storage shows that information could be stored the same way in the universe's matrix.

To be able to observe a single leaf, one has to always come back to the STEM and make his or her way to the leaf, one experience at a time, collapsing Schrodinger's equation one reality at a time. In chapter 5, we have outlined the main idea of quantum superposition, which really represents all the possible states in which a system can be found at the same time. When we choose to observe one particular state of the system, we indeed, mathematically collapse the equation into one and one only possible outcome, choosing one leaf on the tree of life from amongst an almost infinite number of leaves emanating from the STEM. However, it seems that NDErs are capable of seeing the whole tree at once and keeping record of every detail of every single leaf of the tree, with no problem (superposition of states).

How do we collect all the leaves from a scientific point of view? How do we access each leaf and find our way to each one of them, time and time again? I believe we can in a certain way that overcomes the limits of our brain's typical dependence on its five senses.

I have been practicing detachment for a long time in the form for psychic reading, remote viewing and Spiritual Sight.

All my sessions are carefully followed by objective verification of the information I get from a situation, a site, a person (dead or alive), a pet, or an object. It is a motivating step, and is rigorous from a scientific point of view. This is one important step that I take to improve my own skills. The question is: can another person retrieve the same information? In other words, can my first person experience be replicated by a third party for the same information (same leaf)?

In theory, yes, why not. However, because of the very nature of the work it is quite difficult. Another viewer could very well retrieve another piece of information pertaining to the same subject of the reading or the viewing, but not necessarily the same information. There is no particular reason why two viewers would be able to view the same thing. This is not surprising as two or more viewers often disagree about perceptions that they have with the ordinary five senses. We all have a slightly or even profoundly different view of reality, as studies of eyewitness testimony in legal cases has documented. So, it is not surprising that this occurs with our other less developed senses.

Furthermore, despite the fact that two viewers might use the same detachment technique, it is not guaranteed they will access the same information!

Why? Consider the experience of looking at a tree. Can you pinpoint the one leaf that has a tiny dot of red, nestled in the middle of the canopy? Most certainly not! The chances that two or more viewers will pick the same leaf with the same tiny red dot are very slim in fact; like your chances of winning the lottery. So, it is just as unlikely that two or more viewers using Spiritual Sight or other detachment techniques to access their other senses will remote view the same thing.

Does this mean that the very nature of the process prevents scientific replication?

Most serious viewers and readers work from a blank slate, with no front-loading. Front-loading (in the remote viewing world) is the action of receiving information beforehand, about a situation, a person, or an object you are supposed to read or remote view. For example, someone asks a medium to find his lost dog. But the dog owner gives the medium the dog's name, its breed, age, color, and his last known location etc.

Front-loading is dangerous for authenticity and validity because it impedes detachment. And if you don't detach properly, your left-brain and your ego will insidiously take over and will try to interpret the information received beforehand, rather than let the right-brain do its job. Although skeptics often think that mediums use frontloading as a means to do "cold readings", meaning the medium simply uses the front-loaded information to create a final reading, in fact frontloading overshadows the data from the universal consciousness resulting in the medium missing the true information.

So, true viewing or true reading is best done with absolutely zero front-loading, meaning no pre-information is given to the reader or viewer. When I do my readings as a medium, or my sessions with Spiritual Sight, I do not obtain any information about the subject. This means I do not know the age, the sex, or any of the circumstances of a client before I do the reading. The same is true with spiritual sight sessions. I work from a number which is used to identify the remote site or picture of that site that I am then going to describe in tremendous detail.

By not accepting front-loading, mediums and remote viewers position themselves as close as is possible to the conditions of a double-blind experience. (Refusing front-loading is one way of the "double" part of the experiment. The other way is achieved when the recipient of the reading has no knowledge of the reading itself in terms of the day and time it is happening and of its method.)

However, without front loading, it becomes very difficult for two viewers or readers to zero in on the very same piece of information. Both viewers and readers will most certainly find a branch awash with leaves relative to the information they are looking for; but it is probable that as they go deeper into details they might go astray and split onto different paths (different leaves) only to find different information in the end. (The information will be valid in both cases, but totally different from one another.) There can be not enough detachment, and too many leaves to choose from. Replication then becomes a problem. The information exists; we can access it, yet we can't guarantee two people will access the same information on demand. There is so much information around us. Yet, the work of Controlled Remote Viewing and Spiritual Sight shows that this type of replications can still be achieved with a very specific protocol and technique. We will describe in which astonishingly unsuspected environment this has happened, in our chapter 17.

What we can replicate, time and time again though, is the protocol, the detailed method used, which consists of looking for the information and then authenticating it through the work of a third party, when the information is verifiable. In spite of the promising research that I have done, from a scientific standpoint the replication of the retrieval of one specific piece of information from the universal consciousness by a human brain, seems compromised. It is possible and happens "quite often" but not in systematic fashion. This does not satisfy the modern scientific method which often demands laboratory based replication of research. In fact, "quite often" is not a rare thing in all of scientific research. Many research groups have done experiments which have results that "quite often" show a given outcome, but not often enough to constitute incontrovertible scientific evidence. Much of this research is accepted by the scientific community as being scientific fact. This problem is so widespread that it is now termed "the replication crisis". In the physical sciences, as many as 50% of scientists reported failing to replicate other scientists' studies.

Research on the subject though is extremely promising, but "quite often" does not cut it still, in science. However, replication failures are indeed common in all fields of science, so that fact cannot stop us from pursuing promising scientific leads.

As a newly emerging science, consciousness research is not then condemned to navigating within a pseudo-science and philosophy framework forever. Be reassured. In reality, the replication process hasn't really been studied yet.

What has been studied is the retrieval of information followed by its verification, as mentioned above and stressed by professor Gary Schwartz in his *"The Afterlife Experiments"* book.

Gary Schwartz is a professor of psychology, medicine, neurology, psychiatry and surgery at the University of Arizona. His research is one of the first pioneer attempts to study, in a controlled environment, the validation of a firs person experience by a third person or a third party. In the work that he has done with trained psychic mediums, the subjectivity of their first person detachment (psychical) experience is counteracted by a binary system that he puts in place, which aims at verifying the information the mediums come forth with: a 1 if the medium gives correct, authenticated information and a 0 if the information is wrong. A control group carries out the same experiment. At the end, he calculates the number of 1s and the number of 0s and establishes a rate or accuracy well above the 50% chances of getting a 1 or a 0. (The percentage is systematically around 80% of 1s). The group of trained mediums also obtains much better results than the control group, where people have never trained their (right) brain to do such work. In these experiments, he demonstrates that the trained mediums do not obtain the information just by pure chance or by "fishing" it from carefully examining their sitters' faces or demeanor, as each participant in the experiment is isolated physically.

In fact, we have already progressed further than these experiments conducted in 2008. Today, we know that it is possible to retrieve information remotely because our universe is information-theoretic based. Data is everywhere, encoded in the very fabric of the universe, and our brains have a much bigger capability than originally thought, to acquire information.

The next step, which remote viewers around the globe have already achieved, is to demonstrate that two or more people can obtain the same information remotely, upon request. This, as I previously stated, needs replication by other scientists. The ultimate experience will be to create protocols that other scientists can precisely follow and in doing so precisely replicate the experimental design. This has been done with limited success in studies currently in the scientific literature, primarily because the different scientists found it hard to replicate each other's protocols in a precise manner.

We are at the dawn of quantum computers creation. We are trying to create a machine which will possess computing capabilities so extreme and so fast that some scientists say it will be able to replicate "consciousness".

I personally do not believe they are on the right path with this idea. I simply believe consciousness is a whole that is constantly expanding. You cannot create something that already exists. You can only imitate it and add to it. Computers will indeed have the capability of processing consciousness in a revolutionary way, but they will never "create it". Consciousness, although perhaps associated with the creation of the matter of the universe, cannot be created as a function of machine activity, no more than consciousness is the creation of brain activity. The best we could hope for is that a quantum computer might also filter consciousness in the same manner as that a brain or a thermometer does.

Like a brain, computers can only be "aware" of the information. This is why they are made of "hard-ware" and use "soft-wares." They are just a-ware of the information. The etymology of the words ware and aware give us a real sense of what computer and brains are. Ware: *""manufactured goods, goods for sale," Old English waru "article of merchandise," also "protection, guard," hence probably originally "object of care, that which is kept in custody," from Proto-Germanic *waro (source also of Swedish vara, Danish vare, Old Frisian were, Middle Dutch were, Dutch waar, Middle High German, German ware "goods"), from PIE *wer- (4) "to perceive, watch out for" (see ward (n.))."* From: http://www.etymonline.com/index.php?term=ware. Aware: *late Old English gewær, from Proto-Germanic *ga-waraz (source also of Old Saxon giwar, Middle Dutch gheware, Old High German giwar, German gewahr), from *ga-, intensive prefix, + waraz "wary, cautious".* From: http://www.etymonline.com/index.php?allowed_in_frame=0&search=aware

    Computers will always be "goods" that are "wary" of things. But what about the brain then? Brain: *"Old English brægen "brain," from Proto-Germanic *bragnam (source also of Middle Low German bregen, Old Frisian and Dutch brein), from PIE root *mregh-m(n)o- "skull, brain" (source also of Greek brekhmos "front part of the skull, top of the head"). But Liberman writes that brain "has no established cognates outside West Germanic ..." and is not connected to the Greek word. More probably, he writes, its etymon is PIE *bhragno "something broken."* – From http://www.etymonline.com/index.php?term=brain Well, the brain, as it seems, is "something broken" that is "wary and cautious". What broken wary thing could possibly create consciousness? I am joking with a serious point to my word play. My point is what I have already demonstrated, that the brain, be it a computer brain or a human brain, can only filter and process consciousness, but cannot create it.

Brains and computers are merely machines, aware of the information around them and able, to a certain degree, to process it.

Something baffles me however. Our brain seems to be fitted with something extra; a unique power, which machines can't reproduce. Our brain is capable of "feeling" and "knowing" without rationalizing. It can know information, even before the information becomes available locally by our other senses. These are the seventh, eighth and ninth senses, which are not even part of the dialogue concerning thinking computers.

What amazes me even more is that millions of dollars have already been poured into the development of super computers, but little research to none is done to understand why we use so few of our brain capabilities. It is my opinion that this poorly understood "unused" brain capacity is in fact that portion of the brain dedicated to the seventh, eighth and ninth senses.

We are super computers, far more complex than any quantum computer! Up until about 200 000 years ago, the human brain had evolved to satisfy our survival on Earth, and pretty much nothing else. Then the human brain's physiology evolved into what we know of the brain today. About 3000 BC the human brain mastered written language. Still, no significant change has been recorded in its fundamental structure. The brain just learned to use more of its capabilities.

    Written language is one of the biggest cultural advances of our human condition. It is also a double-edged sword as we are limited by language as to what we can think. As we became more proficient in writing and expressing ourselves, we lost touch with the true nature of our reality. Our language is only adapted to our survival and social interactions. The study of the brain, however, reveals that its capabilities go way beyond survival and language.

    There is considerable evidence including the work of Princeton Professor Julian Jaynes that preliterate humans were right-brain dominate and used their extended sensory perceptions far more than literate humans. When we developed the capability of written language and the formation of the independent ego (which is left-brain based), we may have lost much of our innate abilities to obtain and process information directly from the universal consciousness.

    Today, the idea that our brain can grab and process information from our universe in a different manner is no longer a question of survival but one of expansion, the same kind of expansion that one feels during an NDE. Indeed, NDErs report that they do not have the proper language to express what they have felt when they were experiencing clinical death. Similarly, theoretical physicists also have an inability to adequately describe the ultimate reality of the universe. The words we have in our language(s) do not even begin to describe the extent of the expansion both groups have felt during their experiences. As recluse tribes close to the Equator do not have a word for "snow" and people living above the arctic circle have more than twenty-nine words to describe all kinds of snow; and reversely, people living in the cold might not have proper words to describe the Amazon jungle, we are all stuck in our restricted reality, incapable of describing the true information in its entirety, limited by our language and the locality of our five senses.

    Expansion and detachment are what we need to practice in order to grasp the full spectrum of consciousness. This is what I am actively doing as a medium. It requires us to work with our brain in much different ways than the routine processing we subject it to on an everyday basis. It seems however, that once we have established these new neuro-pathways, these information highways become permanent, no different than the permanent neural pathways established by learning to ride a bicycle.

Chapter 14
HOW IS CONSCIOUSNESS PROCESSED THROUGH THE BRAIN?
The cases of cognitively impaired people

"Quiet people have the loudest minds."
– Stephen W. Hawkins

How can we design an experiment to replicate the retrieval of one specific piece of information at a distance?

What is truly a formidable barrier to experimental studies of consciousness is that it is an ever changing, shape-shifting, quantum-like environment, impalpable, untamable and sometimes unfathomable, but is filled with an ever-evolving body of information.

When we think we understand consciousness through philosophy, then science and medicine come to interfere and add new layers of knowledge. Yet when we assume we have penetrated its mystery through rationality, we realize that its manifestations go beyond the activity of the cerebral cortex.

Comatose patients, from brain damage or other reasons, represent an ideal venue to study consciousness. These situations can lead to dramatic stories of hope as well as an understanding that consciousness survives in such tragic settings.

In comatose patients, the cerebral cortex no longer processes sensory information, resulting in a total loss of the manifestation of the person, the ego, the self through the body; a sort of little death of the information-theoretic essence of the person.

The only functions which are preserved often are those basic, innate functions that do not require a voluntary action, such as breathing, or the beating of a heart. In some cases, of course, these functions are also altered and require assistance from medical apparatuses.

Yet many comatose patients who "come back" tell stories that could only be validated if they were totally conscious (in the medical sense of the term) at the time when the stories were happenings.

I personally had a profound experience connecting with such a person, at a distance (he was in Utah and I in Florida). As always, I was unaware of the subject of my reading, so I did not know who he was and why he was in a coma.

During my reading (asked by a family friend to try and see if I could communicate with him), *Dustin (the patient) came to me with many validations of what was happening around him. He described his hospital room to a T, told me when his wife was visiting and then started requesting things to be changed in his room and in the way he was treated. *(The full story of Dustin can be found in my book "God consciousness, The Journey of a Science Driven Psychic Medium", available on Amazon.com).

I AM, THEREFORE I THINK

All these sensory perceptions and requests could only have been made, in theory, by a fully cognizant conscious mind and yet Dustin was in the deepest coma.

This raises an important question. Are patients with Alzheimer's disease or with schizophrenia as "absent" or as "delirious" as they seem to be? With Alzheimer's patients, we could argue that their dysfunctional brain is not allowing them proper communication with their surrounding family and friends, though many accounts of death bed visions tell stories of ultra-lucid minds of the same patients right before the time of death. This clarity of the mind of Alzheimer's patients prior to death is well documented. As for people with schizophrenia, could it be that the wiring of their brains allows them to gather a lot more information than normal, too much information in fact, that they are inadequately built to process? Many psychologists including Julian Jaynes believe this to be the case.

What does this tell us? It tells us that there can be a disconnect between the brain itself and consciousness. The patterns observed in comatose people who later awaken, NDE experiencers, as well as the lucidity documented in Alzheimer's patients prior to death, all is more evidence that the existence of consciousness does not seem to depend on healthy brain functions. Its manifestation might be impaired by a dysfunctional brain, but not its existence.

I believe consciousness is a collection of data, which has accumulated through the whole universe since the first quantum fluctuation appeared out of the quantum vacuum.

Every single being, plant, or element that exists on this Earth is bombarded by the sum total of consciousness. We try to make sense of it using our brain and all sensors we have at our disposal, and it gives us a certain image of what the universe could be. But that image is restricted in multiple ways from the purely physical to the conceptual. For instance, we do not see ultra-violet light. A bee will argue with you that the flower you see as yellow is actually of a nice bright white and a deep red. That is the bee's reality; this is how the bee processes the information. Does it make your reality more valid than the bee's way of seeing the world? Of course, not. The bee's reality is shaped by its brain functions and by its sensory perceptions, which are different from yours.

Yet, there is an ultimate truth. And this ultimate truth is that the universe contains all the information that both you and the bee see differently. That truth is what we call universal consciousness.

An interesting fact that corroborates this universal truth that we can only partially access with our five senses is that many NDErs report seeing colors and hearing music in a light and a resonance that they have never experienced before, as if the bee's and our human's realities were combined with all the other possible truths in an almost infinite explosion of information. Ironically, when we lose our five senses we suddenly can perceive all the colors of the universe that exist, but are blinded by the limitations of our five senses.

The pattern we then see emerging is that, NDE experiencers, remote viewers, cognitively impaired patients and people trained in meditation, lose the functions of their ego, the self, also known as the "interpretive" mind. When this occurs, they gain greater access to the ultimate truth, to the universal information: consciousness as a whole. That access is present all along, but is hidden by the activities of the ego.

Whether you are sleeping, in a coma, or under anesthesia, I believe consciousness is still very much present, just not manifested.

Consciousness is an intrinsic part of the universe, which includes dark matter, dark energy, matter and forces, and it is not logical that its existence relies on the function of a tiny brain sitting in the body of a tiny human being or an even tinier bee, living on a minuscule planet in the middle of nowhere!

The sum total of information, consciousness, that constitutes the universe is interpreted in an infinite number of superposed realities that all co-exist in space-time. The bee's reality at a given moment, is a different reality than yours at the same given moment, and yet, since time and space are all spread out, all the bee's realities and all your realities are true because they all emanate from the same source that contains them all: consciousness.

It all boils down to "interpretation" again. When we are fully aware, we are in a constant state of "interpreting" our surroundings.

However, when we are in a coma, or at the moment of passing, or practicing remote viewing, we seem to cease interpreting the information and appreciate its raw and whole nature.

Chapter 15
DO WE HAVE FREE WILL OVER CONSCIOUSNESS?

"As far as I can see, it's not important that we have free will, just as long as we have the illusion of free will to stop us going mad."
– Alan Moore, writer

The true question is: "Is consciousness passive or active?"

If we regard consciousness simply as a field of data and information, totally spread out in the universe, it would be easy to conclude that consciousness is just the passive sum total of all existing bits of information, just waiting to be "downloaded" by sensors or brains. However, from the point of view of the experiencer, it seems like consciousness can manifest itself and intrude unbidden into that experiencer's reality.

What if we considered consciousness as active data, versus passive data? Let's imagine a concept in which a brain, a sensor or an antenna not only grabs data and processes it, but where the data itself would conversely "reach out" to brains, sensors and antennae in a two-way connection.

This would explain why, in the *Spiritual Sight's method, the experimenter could work from a "site address" which is a random generated number assigned to the subject to be remotely viewed. Information concerning the subject would "come" to the experimenter as much as the experimenter reaches out to the site address. It would also explain why grieving people can "receive" messages from their deceased loved ones. (* *"Spiritual Sight, The Manual"*, see the book that I co-wrote with Dr. Melvin Morse, which is a practical guide for remote viewing.)

As a living being on Earth, we are subjected to gravity, to electro-magnetic fields, and to the weak and strong nuclei forces that hold our atoms. We have no free will over the fundamental forces of the universe. Do we have free will over its existence though? Top physicists say that we are in a participatory universe in which the observer can change the outcome of experimental results. Wouldn't this classify as free will over the existence of the universe? It comes down to: do we have free will in processing consciousness?

The answer is yes and no. We have enough free will or at least the illusion of it, to filter the information that matters to us, through certain parts of our brains (to stop us from going mad). However, we have no control over what information hits us, because it is all spread out around us.

What is the sum total of information that makes consciousness? A collection of data measured in all kinds of different units (energy, forces, light, sounds, and quantum states in superposition). That's why determining a unit of consciousness is extremely difficult. We can only determine units of consciousness being processed (temperature, brain waves, kinetic energy of a converting electron etc...).

As humans, when we observe and measure all these things, using our brain or apparatuses, we in fact measure consciousness's subparts, in different units. But consciousness as a whole remains a mystery.

This is why discovering the Theory of Everything is like finding the Holy Grail. The Theory of Everything (ToE) is a hypothetical unique theory that would unify all aspects of physics in the universe, using one single equation. General relativity, classical physics and quantum mechanics would then all be described by that specific and unique equation.

This is a Dantesque endeavor, which has been haunting every physicist since the discovery of general relativity by Einstein. The Theory of Everything would create a whole, in which everything in the universe would be accounted for. This whole, I believe, is described by the collectiveness of consciousness.

Let's go back for a minute to the idea of consciousness manifesting without being prompted by being processed or measured. What are some examples of this?

Example one: You have no free will over how your body will react to the temperature outside because you are built to react to hot and cold in a certain way. Temperature, being a part of the information of the universe, it has precedence over your own will to react to it.

Example two: You have no free will over how you will be affected by gravity. You can decide to build a rocket to go to space to experience the minimal gravity of space, but in your Earthly disposition you have no free will over how you feel and experience gravity. In other words, you can use your free will to change the gravitational forces you are subjected to, but within a certain gravitational field, you cannot alter the laws of physics that exist in that environment.

Example three: You have no free will over how a nuclear war, thousands of miles away will affect your life. You have free will (at least here in the USA and in all the countries ruled by democracy where human rights are respected) to elect people who might work toward building better foreign relationships that will ultimately make the world a better place. But you have no free will over the head of state who will decide to press the red button, while you are watching the destruction of Earth in disbelief from your living room sofa.

Even more extreme, as mind-boggling as is example three, is example four: believe it or not, you have no free will over consciousness manifesting itself before your eyes, emerging out of thin air. consciousness contains all the characteristics and information pertaining to everything in the universe, including all human beings. It appears that consciousness can "play" the movie of the essence of one particular being, without having this person necessarily filtering or processing her own essence through her body and brain. Consciousness, presenting as a departed loved one, an apparition that we interpret as a friend, or even a person who is still living but is in another place in time or space, can spontaneously appear before any one of us.

Furthermore, a human being's unique consciousness can manifest even after death. Or so it appears. The overwhelming amount of personal experiences with ADC (Spontaneous After Death Communications) is one very striking example of these types of manifestations.

Some ADCs are often spontaneous manifestations of consciousness as they happen without the express request of those to whom they are destined. Yet, manifestations of consciousness are not always spontaneous. 'Paranormal' investigators often provoke this type of communication and use technical equipment that allows them to retrieve bits of information at different degrees of consciousness units, as the initial evidence strongly suggests. However, since their apparatuses are used with the underlying supposition that these manifestations of consciousness can be recorded, and because they don't really know what they are looking for, the results so far are tendentious.

Yet, the numerous observations that are gathered around the world by these investigators (and I am one with them) are the fundamental observations that science uses to create new theories and paradigms. As an example, French farmers documented the stones fell on their fields out of the skies. These observations were at first ignored, but then became too numerous and had to be explained. In turn scientists came up with the understandings that asteroids circle the sun and can fall to this Earth. Other examples include the current widespread use of fluoride to prevent tooth decay which occurred because dentists in naturally fluorinated areas in Texas noted their patients had few cavities. These observations alone do not constitute any kind of scientific proof that we can communicate with deceased people or a specific individual, but the fact that validated information can be gathered without any tangible explanation should be approached with interest and not rejection by the scientific community.

For instance, there are a few concepts that are fundamental precepts of modern physics, which can explain communications with those who have passed, and which come to mind immediately: if an electron can interfere with itself (Ref: the double slit experiment), maybe an entire universe can do the same! We could, for example, envision that two distinct coexisting and expanding universes would interfere with each other and some of the information contained in the consciousness of one universe would poke in the other one, as we see in quantum tunneling effects. This is like the golf ball that can both travel through a wall and be stopped by the wall, that I discussed in chapter 5. Understanding the real-life applications of quantum tunneling effects can explain apparitions and *EVP amongst other types of unexplained manifestations of universal consciousness. *(*EVP: Electronic Voice Phenomena, which are recorded recognizable voices that appear in the context of background of white noise.)*

In a recent talk (IdeaCity 2013), Dr. Geordie Rose, founder of D-Wave, a company specialized in building quantum computers, referred to his middle son who has a teddy bear called "Bear Bear." One night his son became scared and asked to sleep with his older brother. His older brother refused to sleep with him. Dr. Rose then reminded his son that he has "Bear Bear" to comfort him, but his son retorted that "Bear Bear" is not real. Dr. Geordie then understood that when his son said, "he is not real" he really meant "he is not alive."

Dr. Geordie Rose, as many other scientists working in this field, believes "that the power of quantum computing is that we can "exploit parallel universes" to solve problems that we have no other means of confirming." He, as John Wheeler did, understands that this is a participatory universe. We want to believe that there is some sort of objective reality "out there" that we interact with. However, as John Wheeler stated: *"useful as it is to say that the world exists independent of us, that view from the standpoint of quantum physics can no longer be upheld."* Dr. Rose realized that this understanding potentially makes "Bear Bear" as real and alive as his son would want him to be.

If quantum computers have the ability to access different states of a particular piece of information at what appears to be the same time from our viewpoint at the classical level of physics, one can legitimately speculate that we humans have the same capability. We simply don't know yet how to harvest the information in a quantum way. The electrical impulses of our neuron pathways will never beat quantum teleportation speed or quantum nonlocality, or maybe the way we have been using our brain, in survival mode, is the reason why we cannot process on a daily basis a broader amount of information in a quantum way. Quantum nonlocality is simply a scientific term representing the idea that in the quantum world, especially in a system, which is entangled (where particles are dependent of one another in that system), pairs (or groups) of particles in this system, regardless of the physical distance between them, seem to yield a bigger probability to be observed in the exact same state for both particles, when one particle of that system is observed. One particle in the system is measured at a certain level or in a certain state and instantaneously, the other(s) particle(s) shows the same level or appears in the same state, even though the other particle(s) hasn't been observed, and thus affected by the measurement.

It is of interest that scientists at the Max Plank Institute in Germany have documented that many aspects of human cognition do in fact function in a quantum nonlocal manner, indication that in theory we can interact with quantum nonlocality. To experience quantum nonlocality in our higher state of awareness would imply that somehow, we are capable of entangling ourselves with the subject(s) of our meditation or readings (for a medium), and thus react the way our subject reacts while being observed. (This could explain, for example, the feeling of physical pain or the precise emotions about a subject, a medium could feel during a reading).

This is why example four is not so much a matter of not having free will in the manifestation of consciousness but more so a statement of our ability to access the information in different states at the same time.

For example, consciousness contains the information of Albert Einstein being dead and also the information of Albert Einstein being alive in many different realities. We can exert our free will and try to access all that information about Albert Einstein at once. This is what a remote viewer or psychic medium or a person going through an NDE does. When we stay in the reality we are aware of, through our first five senses, then only one state or another is valid at a given time (time as perceived by us), but not all of them.

Until now, evolution has imprisoned us in the narrow jail of the "survival brain". But the power of the brain put to the task of accessing the diversity of states of everything in the universe is probably the most important scientific discovery that will be made in the next fifty years.

Our brain has helped us thrive on Earth by emphasizing the development of our survival skills. Only a little time has passed, barely a few thousand years, since we have no longer had to focus on day to day survival. In that short time from the viewpoint of the totality of human evolution, we have seen a rapid cultural evolution. We have seen how different portions of our brain have developed to give us a different perspective on our surroundings without necessarily triggering any change in the physiology of our brain. One example is the restructuring of our brain to permit written language, which has only evolved in the past 5000 years. We can anticipate considerable more restructuring or discovering unused skills in the development of our advanced senses.

In order to make my point I am going to wrap up my thread in color: In survival mode, our brain sees red as blood, anger as a response to danger, green as forest for protection, blue as water and sky for life, and yellow as sun and fire for heat. Our brain today (and for the last few thousand years in our evolutionary history) has evolved into being able to differentiate all kinds of shades of red, and all kinds of shades of green, blue, and yellow, which are not necessarily useful for survival but have a deep impact on how we perceive the world. These shades of colors existed before. Our brain had the necessary capacity to apprehend them, but hadn't created the pathways to use them because our survival was not at stake. The red perceptual system worked well to sense the presence of danger but did not describe a rare flower with a velvety crimson shade that would only be found in exotic places and thus would become so precious to us. We simply did not have the time or inclination to access these other states of understanding even though, they had always been here. We were only trying to survive.

In conclusion, in some ways, we do have the free will to access different states of existence and to grasp a much higher level of the complexity of things. Yet, we are only beginning to understand the capacities of our brain, as well as what creates its own limitations.

Free will is what will always differentiate us from super quantum computers. Computer algorithms can simulate free will, but they will never be able to create it because, by definition, if computers need programs to manifest free will, then it's not free will! We are part of the co-creation of the universe; we evolve because we are part of the universe and it is contained within us. That paradoxical statement of human existence is what computers will never achieve.

Chapter 16
IS CONSCIOUSNESS RESPONSIBLE FOR ALL THE DEEDS AND EVENTS IN THE UNIVERSE(S) AND ON EARTH?

"We seek to uncover, behind the events, changes in the collective consciousness. We reject wholesale references to the "spontaneity" of the movement, references which in most cases explain nothing and teach nobody. Revolutions take place according to certain laws. This does not mean that the masses in action are aware of the laws of revolution, but it does mean that the changes in mass consciousness are not accidental, but are subject to an objective necessity which is capable of theoretic explanation, and thus makes both prophecy and leadership possible."
— Leon Trotsky, History of the Russian Revolution

I believe consciousness is to our earthly world what quantum reality is to classical physics; the sum total of all possibilities and all information in every possible state, that can only be partially interpreted through the restrictive lens of our five senses.

If we consider that all time has been spread out since the beginning of the universe and that consciousness has been expanding since that moment, inevitably data and information about events within consciousness are superposed in the same space-time. consciousness fills the available space-time with more information and more data at any given time. It expands, yet is contained.

How can something expand to virtually no limit in a contained space-time?

Maybe because each event is part of a single universe. The expansion of consciousness might then be contingent upon the superposition of all events in a quantum way. Let's map this with the different types of universe interpretations that we reviewed in chapter 4. (Fig. 7) represents consciousness expanding and containing multiple universes superposed at each and every moment of the expansion.

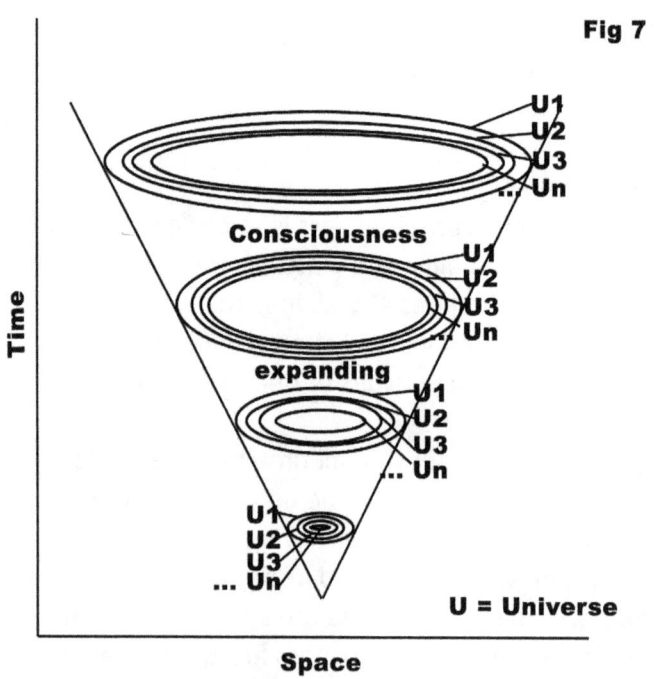

Fig 7

(Fig. 8) would explore the Wheeler-DeWitt interpretation of the universe where all time is spread out. However, each person within each universe, feels that time and space are linear. All the universes are in superposed states within consciousness.

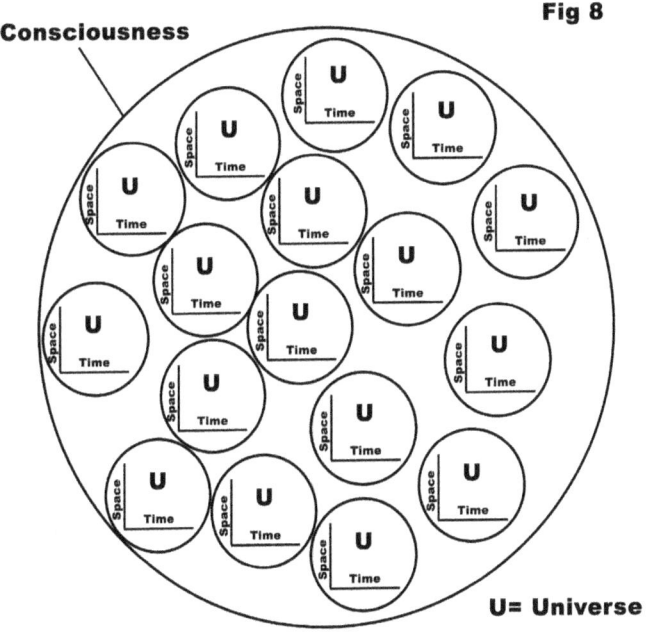

Fig 8

U= Universe

Are all events already laid out in the universe as single dots in the space-time-consciousness continuum? Do we still have an action on our own destiny? Antoine de Lavoisier, a French chemist of the 18th century, once said, *"nothing is created, nothing's lost, everything changes to another form."* If everything that we see, is everything there is, in our immediate external world, our referential, the fact that we are in a specific universe here on Earth with religious wars raging in the Middle East, for example, is just one of the many states of existence of the universe within the whole of consciousness.

Yet, as we act and react within our surroundings we transform and expand the data associated with our actions.

I have little to no doubt that there is another universe in which all nations on Earth are living peacefully. That kind of makes me a bit jealous not being immediately aware of this other universe, where I certainly live too!

Information, as consciousness, might be the only thing in the whole universe that is actually expanding by adding to itself like a feedback loop, feeding all the universes in superposition.

None of these ideas about consciousness are supported by mathematical equations, or a philosophical precept, but they can't be denied just because we haven't computed them yet. Or have we? Theoretical physicists candidly admit that they have no words to explain the reality that their mathematical equations define, yet an increasing number of them state that their mathematical equations define and explicate what we call consciousness.

Consciousness as a whole clearly plays a preponderant and anonymous role in our choices of action without hindering our free will.

Consciousness is the silent witness of our evolution within the specific universe we live in. It lets us borrow from its infinite data bank on an everyday basis to help us make decisions and to allow us to evolve. In exchange, our actions are "written" in this bank as new information readily available to be downloaded. Thus, the balance remains even as consciousness still expands.

Like our planet, which evolves at an almost imperceptible rate to us, consciousness acts upon things and beings in the same way. Everyday our collective consciousness acts upon itself, unbeknownst to us, unless we examine it closely. In the same fashion that we are not really aware of the drift of the continents unless we actually measure it, we cannot readily see how consciousness acts upon everything in the universe unless we pay close attention to it. The actions of consciousness' collective processing are most often imperceptible to us, at our human level, like the exchanges of energy are at the subatomic level. But their effects are measurable and show real global interactions, regardless of how subtle.

Luckily, a few scientists, always pioneers and always initially contested by the scientific establishment, have found ways to witness these imperceptible interactions, be they subatomic ones or our interactions with universal consciousness. For example, the effects of collective intentional thoughts have been measured by their influence of the random output of true random events generators (REGs). One such pioneer, Dr. Robert Jahn was Dean of Engineering at Princeton University when the PEAR (Princeton Engineering Anomaly Research Lab) program was launched in 1979. This program aimed at studying psi phenomena and global consciousness effects on our world. Dr. Roger Nelson, who served as the coordinator of experimental work at (PEAR) and Dr. Robert Jahn conducted many experiments involving collective consciousness and REGs. The original program, though considered controversial, lasted over twenty-eight years and was terminated in 2007. For many old-school scientists, remote viewing and psi phenomena are like Plato's prisoner coming back from outside blinded by the light; they present a challenge to the establishment invested in the materialistic philosophical understanding of reality and an "embarrassment" to a university's academic reputation.

Nevertheless, Dr. Roger Nelson carried on the mission to explore consciousness, as the director of the Global Consciousness Project (GCP), a multi-lab association dedicated to research on collective consciousness processing and its potential actions on the world.

Since 1998, Dr. Nelson and his team have tirelessly shown evidence of deviations in the randomness of the output of REGs which are associated with major events in the world such as the funeral of Lady Diana, a world cup finale, or the 9/11 tragedy to name just a few.

The randomness of data generated by the REGs seems to shift to a perceptible non-random behavior and even recognizable patterns which appear when a collective event happens anywhere on our planet. Obviously, the results have been challenged many times by other scientists who keep stating that the protocols and methodology of research are not strong enough to suggest evidence of global consciousness interaction on the world. Such is the scientific method and the proper path to the coming shift in the scientific world view from its current materialistic philosophy to a consciousness based paradigm.

What a breath of fresh air it would be if the community of scientists stuck in their reactionary rebuttal mode started working together with those they harshly criticize. They act like Plato's prisoners who only believe in the shadows they see on the walls of their own created prisons. It has been said of the major scientific paradigm shifts in the past that the guardians of the old paradigm have to die off before the new paradigm can be established.

With what I can gather, it seems to me that we do have a role singularly and collectively in the building of our own universe, at least right here on Earth. For the rest of the universe, and that's a big chunk, consciousness units might be measured in a different manner, yet allowing every single particle to exist and evolve.

Singularly and collectively, my theory based on my own personal experiments as well as the aforementioned review of the scientific literature is that every single object in the universe hails from consciousness while creating it.

Chapter 17
CAN CONSCIOUSNESS HEAL THE WORLD?

"Heal the world
Make it a better place
For you and for me
And the entire human race
There are people dying
If you care enough for the living
Make it a better place
For you and for me"
— Michael Jackson, "Heal the World"

Consciousness seems to be the egg and the chicken all together. It gives birth to our universe (or universes) and yet expands from its own intentions. No computer on Earth would be able to have the same impact on its surrounding. Even if you programmed tens of thousands of quantum computers to react the same way to the processing of a world event, I honestly doubt that REGs would be affected by their results. So far, no computer has been shown to have any effect on a random event generator. My opinion is that we have something different and something very special as sentient beings. Machines will never be able to create or emulate that "something," only simulate it.

The fact that we are capable of emotions catapults us to a whole different level. Sure, we don't have the capabilities and the computing speed of a quantum computer. Neither do we have the power to solve (in a record time) scientific puzzles; but what quantum computers will never have, is the ability to "feel" a situation.

And I am not talking about our five senses, because a computer can be fitted with many types of sensors that would replicate "live" senses. I am referring to the "feeling" that compels you to choose one solution over another, not because there is a logical explanation to your choice, but because you just feel it's the right thing to do. These are our advanced senses that I discussed earlier.

When Max Tegmark says, "consciousness is what information feels when being processed," I think he might have it reversed; as it seems that consciousness exists whether we manifest it or not. In my view, I'd rather say that consciousness is not "what it feels like when information is processed," but that "feeling is what allows the whole of consciousness i.e. information to be processed."

I truly don't think quantum computers will ever be able to do that.

When inmates, beginner remote viewers sitting in state prison cells (and I am not talking about Plato's cave, but about real prisoners this time, serving their time in a correctional facility in Delaware), described the essence of a photo hidden in a sealed envelope they've been given to remote view blindly, their lives were forever altered. Their processing of consciousness is altered and their projection of themselves into collective consciousness is profoundly and positively changed.

For almost three years (2013-2016), I have worked with Dr. Melvin Morse (best-selling author of "Closer to the Light") on broadening the horizon of close to twenty inmates, incarcerated at the Sussex Correctional Institution in Delaware, with the teaching of Spiritual Sight. Spiritual Sight is a combined technique of remote viewing and spirituality that Dr. Morse and I have refined during these years, and which has "real" applications in the "real" world.

The method draws its basis from the remote viewing technique set by the Stargate project, and expands from the Buddhist philosophy on the ideas of meditation and compassion.

The Stargate project was born in the 1970's as a controlled remote viewing (CRV) experiment. It aimed, secretly, in the middle of the Cold War, at competing with the Soviet equivalent of the same area of research. The idea was to control the enemy by getting access to their military intelligence through the work of ESP (Extra Sensory Perception). The military program was run over a period of almost twenty years by the CIA and the DIA and was decommissioned in 1995. Because of the real-world applications of this psychic spy program, it continues to present day, funded by various government agencies.

As a result of this classified information being placed in the public domain, there has been a growing interest in CRV by all kinds of enthusiasts around the world. The infatuation with the idea (more than for its true noble possibilities) has led to the formation of a close-knit community of people, who sometimes thinks they "own" not only the technique, but also the ability, the knowledge and the right to disseminate the method. This ego-based treatment of a natural human ability is a bit frustrating, as many people in that community treats the work more as a way of making themselves look like they are part of some sort of elite, rather than as a way of truly advancing not only science, but more so our humanity.

There is also a tendency to treat the results of remote viewing as trophies. Of course, we all have a propensity to, once in a while, act foolishly and cockily when we feel there is support and acknowledgement for our success. Everyone in the field has been guilty of that habit!

Let's face it, whether you have been doing this work two days or ten years, if you "hit the target," meaning if you perfectly describe a remote site, blind to you, with all its physical and emotional attributes, you feel like the king of the world. This feeling of "nailing the target" goes from complete disbelief for the beginners to necessary reassurance for the habitual practitioner. Once you do this work often, your ego can indeed get in the way and throw curveballs at you in the form of anxiety of failure to identify the target or excessive pride in one's abilities.

Dr. Melvin Morse and I have developed a technique based on controlled remote viewing known as Spiritual Sight. It allows the practitioner to use the teaching of ancient philosophies such as Buddhism and Hinduism, and apply them to modern techniques of remote viewing in order to maximize the results in a record time. Furthermore, as it is an advanced meditative technique primarily designed to foster spiritual understandings, it often avoids the egotism and pride seen in simple remote viewing, which I mentioned earlier.

I used to think that I needed a very quiet environment and special conditions to sit down and do a remote viewing session or a mediumship session. While these preparatory actions certainly help to yield a great session, the work Dr. Melvin Morse has done with inmates proves that it might not be a necessity. The inmates that he worked with performed in an environment of constant noise, hostility and anger in the background.

I also used to think that the more we train, the better we become. While a good long training does not typically hurt anyone, its main goal is not to get "better at remote viewing" but to acquire more direct pathways to achieve the state of consciousness we need to be in, in order to retrieve remote information. However, once we have acquired these pathways, they are imprinted forever like knowing how to ride a bike, and thus do not require further learning, just "maintenance" practice. As Buddhism teaches, once we use a ferry to cross the river to the other side, the ferry is no longer necessary.

The first reaction of inmates presented with the idea of remote viewing a photo in a sealed envelope was direct rejection. Yet once they were convinced to try just "for the fun of it" most of those men who did try found themselves in complete disbelief when they compared their "viewing" and the image ultimately revealed to them post session. That is the first step, the trophy result! For many of the men, it was the first time that they succeeded in doing anything of a spiritual nature.

Indeed, the first reaction of an inmate to whom a sealed envelope is given, being asked to perceive what's in it without opening it, is one of incredulity. At the most, mockery ensues. Yet, when the initial embarrassment dissipates, pride takes over; then pushed by the determination that only a man confined in a $10m^2$ cell twenty-three hours a day can have, the inmate becomes game for it. If the session is unsuccessful, he will simply mock the idea saying that he knew this was complete "B.S.", and thus will not lose face, but if the inmate succeeds, he will come out of it a "boss".

In reality, the results of the first sessions with several inmates did inspire in them total incredulity. *"They are so spot on and so detailed. When the photos, hidden in the envelopes are revealed to them, the expression on their faces is one of total perplexity, as if someone had played a trick on them,"* reports Dr. Morse. It's a trophy result, which I previously described as occurring in the remote viewing community who learned their techniques from declassified documents from the CIA. However, with spiritual sight, they quickly moved beyond pride and ego, and understood the deeper implications of their results with regards to our connection to universal consciousness, that source of love referred by Pope Francis.

To realize the scope of such a research, one has to really be aware of the daily climate that permeates a state prison, which is not one of calm and serenity. There are constant loud noises that resonate in the entire facility, interspersed with discussions and screams from altercations. There is no way to isolate oneself and to avoid the brouhaha and the constant taunting. An inmate who dares to sit down and try to meditate, let alone "remote view", is often the subject of teasing from the other inmates who would surround him and his mentor with loud laughs or pushes and shoves.

Yet, the repeated efforts of these inmates, who have given a shot or two at Spiritual Sight under those conditions, and in that environment, have been repaid with extraordinary results. The results are not only the trophy type – that of hitting the target. Though matching results constitute an immediately rewarding part of the process, something inmates haven't been accustomed to very often while in jail, it seems to have a much more profound impact on their psyche.

Though the experiments that Dr. Morse has led in prison are not scientifically controlled and were not conducted in a laboratory environment, they constitute nevertheless a very firm basis for further research. He and I developed a consistent protocol for the experiments. I sent in to the prison sealed envelopes with the pictures to be viewed during the sessions; sealed so that neither Dr. Morse nor the inmates knew what the picture was until the end of the session. It is astonishing that these men who were unlikely candidates to perform at the same spiritual level as Tibetan monks or CIA trained psychics were able to achieve any results at all, much less the often jaw dropping results that they achieved.

The subtext of the research is described as follows: "Can consciousness heal the world?" This is because so many remarkable transformations in character occurred to the men who were successful at Spiritual Sight sessions; they were often healed of past traumas and angers.

Is the revelation that we can access information through different parts of our brain and "feel" connected with everything, a motivation for bettering our own humanity? If inmates, who have been convicted of drug dealing, robbery, child abuse, aggravated assault, fraud, and even murder can connect the dots and realize that their actions are linked to the rest of the world, shouldn't we be teaching Spiritual Sight to all of them? Better yet, shouldn't we be teaching Spiritual Sight to all children, at home, in school before some of them turn into potential criminals?

Shouldn't we be preoccupied by the fact that while giving our children the tools for material survival, we should also give them the tools for spiritual survival in this constant shapeshifting universe? And by spiritual survival I absolutely do not mean religious teaching but survival of the nature and the health of our spirit, our consciousness.

Recently, I was talking to a person who had lost his job and had become depressed. Listening to him, I realized that the most damaging fact to him was not the loss of the job in itself, but the "uncertainty" that he had to face in pursuing the multitude of potential opportunities ahead of him. As I reflect today on the loss of my own father, I concur with the feeling of uncertainty. Losing something or someone dear opens up the prospect of many new outcomes of life, which for a moment (sometimes a long moment) puts us in a state of uncertainty.

This makes me understand the beauty of the universe and of our making. In wanting to be in a world where we could have all the jobs we wanted or be with all our lost loved ones at all time, we do not foresee that it would be totally unlivable. To be in a constant state of quantum superposition where all the outcomes of our life are readily available to us without one definite direction being chosen, would immerse us into a complete and perpetual state of uncertainty. We would not be able to function at our human level.

Nature has built us exactly the way we need to be built in order to live to the fullest our purpose. Yet, it does not mean we cannot get a glimpse of what lies in the collective of consciousness and spend a few Earthly minutes meditating each day to reach out to it to be reassured that, whatever path we are on, it is the right outcome for us, right now.

The indeterministic nature of our collective consciousness is literally a pool of knowledge and information from which we can draw inspiration and encouragement, but which allows us to always return to our 3D reality each time, like Francis Weber's Thanatonauts, or NDErs do, without fearing to lose ourselves in the process.

For inmates, it is the discovery that they are where they are because it is the outcome that they picked or that was picked for them, while faced with other choices in the past. Yet it is also the understanding that other outcomes are possible and that we can have access to these life possibilities by meditating and drawing inspiration from our time connecting with consciousness. Such an inspirational influx came into the mind of one of the inmates to whom Dr. Morse taught Spiritual Sight. This particular person found the courage to pursue the reopening of his case and was able, by himself, to prove his innocence! He was freed immediately.

The true philosophy of life is not dependent on our belief system or our propensity in computing everything into a mathematical equation. It is directly the result of our own actions and our own experience with consciousness. It is the use we make of the only tool we have to figure out who we are: our brain.

Chapter 18
I AM, THEREFORE I THINK

"If the rate of change on the outside exceeds the rate of change in the inside, the end is near."
— Jack Welch, business executive, author, and chemical engineer. Ex-chairman and CEO of General Electric.

Our world is rapidly changing, in so many ways. The dynamics that once ruled commerce have dramatically reverted back to the survival of the fittest; from mutually beneficial win-win relationships, to a race to be a leader. The power relations between countries have increased in intensity because of inequalities and lack of opportunities, yielding to fanaticism and extreme politics of indoctrination.

I feel It is urgent we start changing from the inside. We are still reacting to situations the way we would have centuries ago. We are still blaming our neighbors, our differences. We are still using religious weapons to instill fear. As Gandhi said" Be the change that you want to see".

Our universe is the perfect example of adaptation. In constant shapeshifting action, the universe is the scene of perpetual destruction, and rebirth, while expanding.

We still haven't mastered the art of expansion. Not expansion through power and money, but expansion through our connection with one another.

Quantum mechanics teaches us that all is interconnected. General relativity and cosmology teach us that we are in a universe where all space and time already exist. Spiritual Sight shows us that we can have an objective and true outside view, a true connection with universal consciousness that gives us a new perspective on life. Sometimes having an outside, or a bird's eye view is as simple as taking a backseat and just "looking" without "looking for." One anecdote will help you understand what I mean. The other day, I was looking for the dental floss in my bathroom. It's a small plastic box, square and blue containing a little reel of thread. It's usually either on my husband's sink, or mine. I couldn't find it. I looked and looked to no avail. It's only when I decided to give up and took a step back to leave the bathroom, that a blue patch on the ledge of the bathtub caught my eye. There was the floss, sitting right between the two sinks, directly in front of me. It had been sitting there the whole time I was looking for it. Going from one sink to another, I had passed it many times. Yet, because my left-brain had been telling me it should be on a sink all this time, I had never paid attention to anything else.

A bird's eye view is not only a global view of things, but a view detached from prejudice as we saw it in our previous chapters as well. What does science have to do to come to terms with in this new paradigm? With the fact that looking for something is not always looking at where it's supposed to be.

Expanding our perceptions is the key to the next chapter of scientific exploration.

Consciousness is the reason why everything exists, including the reason why we exist. consciousness is the "I am." The way we process and use consciousness creates the way we interpret the universe we live in. It manifests the "I think." As mathematical as the universe could be, its real nature lies in the unfiltered information that makes our collective consciousness. Simply put, "I am" already exists in our collective consciousness. "I think" only brings forth "I am" but does not create it. Both science and religions are just two different interpretations of that exact same reality. Science finds a similar conclusion as the one found in the Bible, Exodus 3:14:
"God said to Moses, "I AM WHO I AM." And he said, "Say this to the people of Israel: "I AM has sent me to you."""

Whether we decide to call consciousness God, or information, or the Hidden Veiled Reality, we need to understand that, we have the capabilities in us to understand our universe in a much richer and fulfilling way than what we have done until now.

We do not need leaders to do it; we do not need religious doctrines to achieve it, because "I am", our true universal self already knows it all.

It is time we operate the necessary shift in our lives to welcome the fast changes in our humanity, by reversing the "I think, therefore I am" into "I am, therefore I think." Once we understand that we don't have to affirm our ego to be, because we already are, we will be able to reorganize our thought processes. We will then be able to create a better base for our expansion within consciousness, trickling down on our understanding of the universe and thus igniting an explosion of scientific discoveries.

As you may have noticed, this book started by challenging your left-brain a little, your survival preoccupied rational brain, the brain that needs and wants answers and logical explanations.

You might have also noticed how easy it was to shift from challenging that brain to honoring your other brain, your right-brain, the one that understands the necessity of being connected to others and everything.

Science exercises curiosity to ask questions and seek answers about the universe. It is only the byproduct of our human condition, the "I think."

Detachment helps us to acquire a bird's eye view of our universe, because we are it, the "I am."

In detachment, there is expansion. In expansion, there is the notion of globalism. In globalism, there is understanding, altruism, and empathy without the necessity of explanation.

These concepts are the ones we need to master in order to shift from "I think, therefore I am" to

"I am, therefore I think."

My Dad Jean Chauffeton worked with Professor Maurice de Broglie (brother of Louis de Broglie one of the forefathers of quantum mechanics) at the Diderot University with a team of physicists on Wilson Chamber experiments.

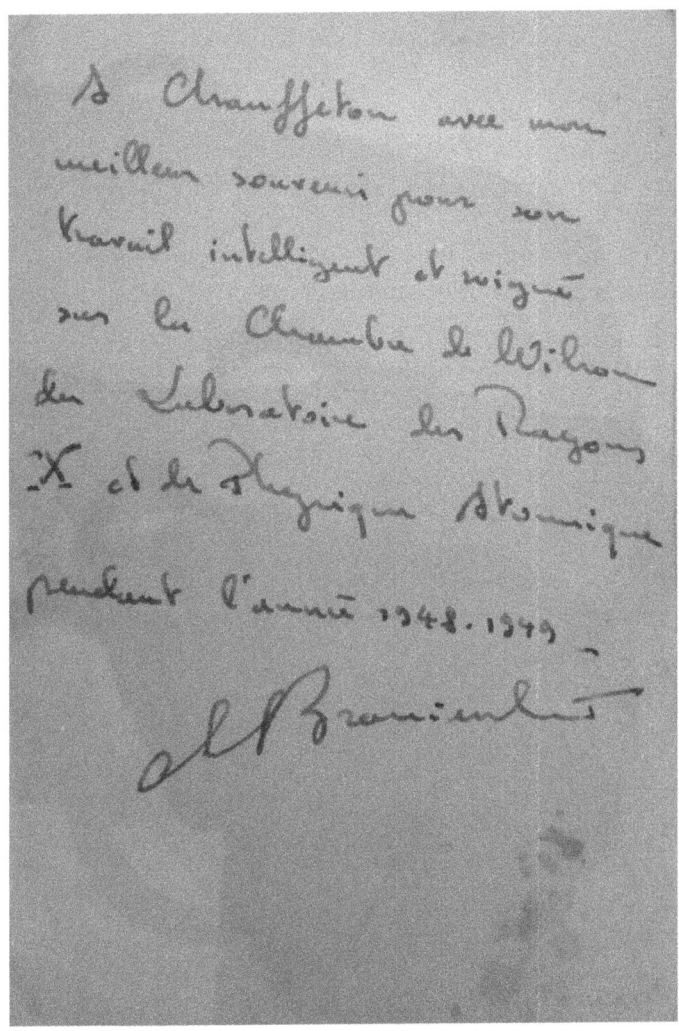

Back of photo signed by the leader of the physicist team at Diderot University and dedicated to my Dad.
It reads:
"To Chauffeton with my token of appreciation for his carefully executed and intelligent work on the X-Ray and particle physics lab's Wilson Chamber during the year 1948/1949"

Bibliography and sources used in this book

The interpretation of quantum mechanics. "Many Worlds or Many Words" by Max Tegmark
http://arxiv.org/pdf/quant-ph/9709032v1.pdf

The Mathematical universe – Book by Max Tegmark) Published by Knopf Random House

Quantum Superposition of States and Decoherence Université Paris Sud / CNRS / PALM
https://www.youtube.com/watch?v=tAIC-FkE2rs

The Pilot Wave Dynamics of Walking Droplets
https://www.youtube.com/watch?v=tAIC-FkE2rs

Quantification en Physique Quantique Animation (Animation in French)
https://commons.wikimedia.org/wiki/File:Quantification_en_physique_quantique.ogv

New Quantum Reality
http://www.wired.com/2014/06/the-new-quantum-reality/

Les 7 merveilles de la Mecanique Quantique (text in French)
https://sciencetonnante.wordpress.com/2013/09/30/les-7-merveilles-de-la-mecanique-quantique/

The Cosmic universe, The Origin of the universe
http://www.faculty.umb.edu/gary_zabel/Courses/Parallel%20universes/Texts/Cosmology,%20Quantum%20Gravity,%20and%20the%20Arrow%20of%20Time.htm

World Science University – Lecture by Andrei Linde Cosmologist.
Lecture "Chaotic Inflation"
http://www.worldscienceu.com/courses/13/elements/oJIQPt

"A participatory universe of J.A Wheeler as an Intentional Correlate of Embodied Subjects and an Example of Purposiveness in Physics"
Alexei V. Nesteruk
http://arxiv.org/pdf/1304.2277v1.pdf

Is the Big Bang defined before or after inflation?
http://physics.stackexchange.com/questions/132794/is-the-big-bang-defined-as-before-or-after-inflation

Galilean Transformation Equations for velocity
https://www.youtube.com/watch?v=NH3_lIkSB9s

What is singularity?
http://www.physlink.com/education/AskExperts/ae251.cfm

Indeterminism and determinism in quantum mechanics
http://link.springer.com/chapter/10.1007%2F978-3-540-70626-7_96

The path integral formulation of quantum theory
http://www.einstein-online.info/spotlights/path_integrals

Fluid Analog in quantum mechanics
https://en.wikipedia.org/wiki/Fluid_analogs_in_quantum_mechanics

Hidden Variable Theory
https://en.wikipedia.org/wiki/Hidden_variable_theory

Copenhagen interpretation
https://en.wikipedia.org/wiki/Copenhagen_interpretation

Neuroscience's new consciousness theory is spiritual
http://www.huffingtonpost.com/bobby-azarian/post_10079_b_8160914.html?

Ontological Arguments
http://plato.stanford.edu/entries/ontological-arguments/

Minkowski space
https://en.wikipedia.org/wiki/Minkowski_space

Help me understand – Friedmann Equation
http://www.sciencechatforum.com/viewtopic.php?t=5200

Diagram of the Evolution of the universe
https://en.wikipedia.org/wiki/Chronology_of_the_universe#/media/File:CMB_Timeline300_no_WMAP.jpg

Chronology of the universe
https://en.wikipedia.org/wiki/Chronology_of_the_universe

Reviewing Friedmann Equation and Inflation Theory by Sub Quantum Energy
http://gsjournal.net/Science-Journals/Research%20Papers-Astrophysics/Download/5534

The Big Bang, common misconceptions
http://angryastronomer.blogspot.com/2006/07/big-bang-common-misconceptions.html

How could the universe expand faster than the speed of light? That seems impossible!
http://scienceline.org/2007/07/ask-romero-speedoflight/

Cosmic Microwave Background (CMB)
https://en.wikipedia.org/wiki/Cosmic_microwave_background

Evidence for Inflation
http://www.counterbalance.org/cq-guth/evide-frame.html

Cosmic Inflation
http://www.physicsoftheuniverse.com/topics_bigbang_inflation.html

What is Gaia Theory?
http://www.gaiatheory.org/overview/

consciousness can be quantified – video Michio Kaku
https://www.youtube.com/watch?v=0GS2rxROcPo

Spiritual Sight, The Manual – Book by Dr. Melvin Morse and Isabelle Chauffeton Saavedra. Available on Amazon.com

God consciousness, The Journey of a Science Driven Psychic Medium – Book by Isabelle Chauffeton Saavedra. Available on Amazon.com

The Tao of Physics – Book by Fritjof Capra (quotes from page 212 and page 222)

La plénitude du vide – Book (in French) by Trinh Xuan Thuan published by Albin Michel

About the Author

Fascinated from an early age by all things related to physics and mathematics, this was Isabelle Chauffeton Saavedra's chosen path when she first began her undergraduate studies in her native France.

Her intended career took an unexpected turn when she found herself in a position of first managing, then owning several businesses across three continents, over an eighteen-year span.

As she returns today to her original passion, Isabelle has set herself apart from many others in what is considered a media-driven and sensationalized area of study, the area of psychic experimentalism. Isabelle strives to promote a respectful and ethical environment within this specific realm of research.

Isabelle's readings are considered double-blind experiments. Additionally, she teaches Spiritual Sight, a method derived from Controlled Remote Viewing. Her most recent partnering research has involved the teaching of Spiritual Sight as a transformational tool, to prison inmates via the insider work of Dr. Melvin Morse.

This is Ms. Chauffeton Saavedra's third book. Previous books include: "God consciousness, The Journey of a Science Driven Psychic Medium" and "Spiritual Sight, The Manual" which she co-authored with Dr. Melvin Morse.

Other passions of Ms. Chauffeton Saavedra include: music, both singing and songwriting.

Isabelle Chauffeton Saavedra can be found on Facebook under her own name, and also administers a website, www.survivalofconsciousness.com where you can find information, blog entries, and set up private readings.

www.ingramcontent.com/pod-product-compliance
Lightning Source LLC
Chambersburg PA
CBHW060528100426
42743CB00009B/1460